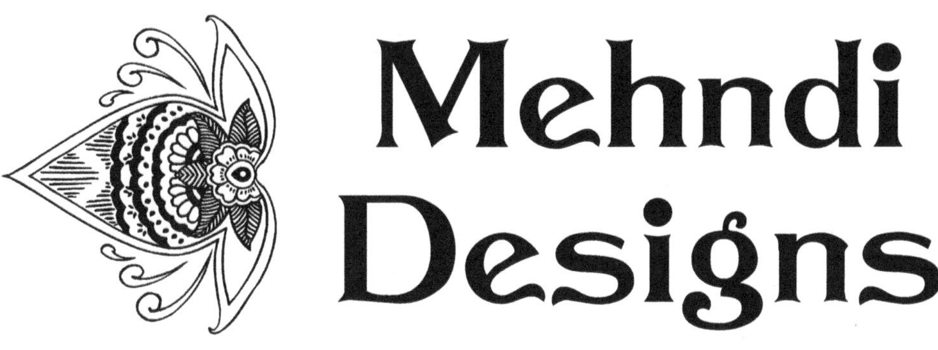

Mehndi Designs

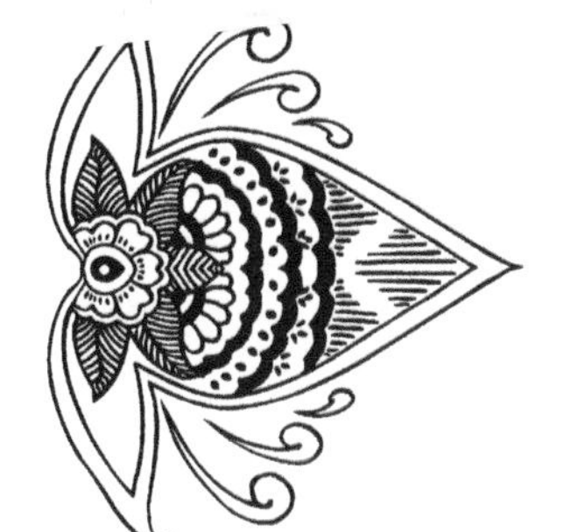

Traditional Henna Body Art

MARTY NOBLE

DOVER PUBLICATIONS
Garden City, New York

Publisher's Note

MEHNDI is the traditional art of henna body painting in India and the Middle East. In India, the temporary designs are usually applied to a woman's hands and feet, but for special occasions, men may also wear them. (At weddings, both bride and bridegroom may be decorated, and often others in the wedding party as well.) As you can see in this collection by artist Marty Noble, the designs are often gloriously attractive. The mehndi artists work with a dye made from dried, ground henna leaves (sometimes with an admixture of various other ingredients, such as tea, coffee, lemon, wine, sugar syrup, egg, yogurt, tamarind, fenugreek seeds, cloves, or titanium powder). The results look for all the world like intricate tattoos—but with the advantage of not demanding a lifelong commitment. Unlike tattoos, mehndi designs generally last no longer than two to four weeks.

Mehndi Designs: Traditional Henna Body Art is a new work, first published by Dover Publications in 2004.

Library of Congress Cataloging-in-Publication Data

Noble, Marty, 1948-
Mehndi designs : traditional henna body art / Marty Noble.
p. cm. — (Dover pictorial archive series)
ISBN-13: 978-0-486-43860-3 (pbk.)
ISBN-10: 0-486-43860-0 (pbk.)
1. Mehndi (Body painting)—Themes, motives. 2. Henna. 3. Stencil work. I. Title. II. Series.

GT2343.N63 2004
391.6—dc22

2004050047

Printed in the United States of America
43860015 2025
www.doverpublications.com

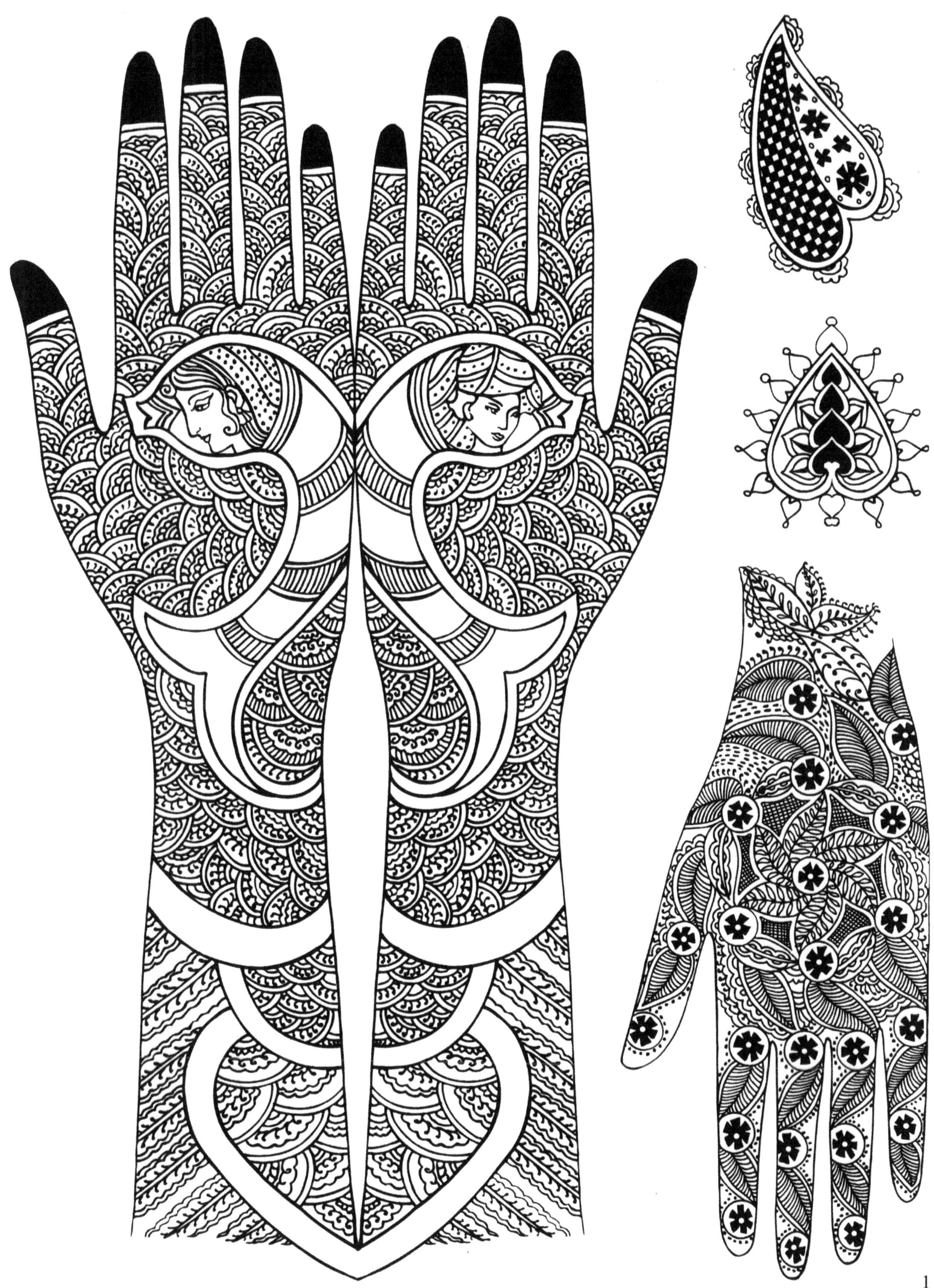

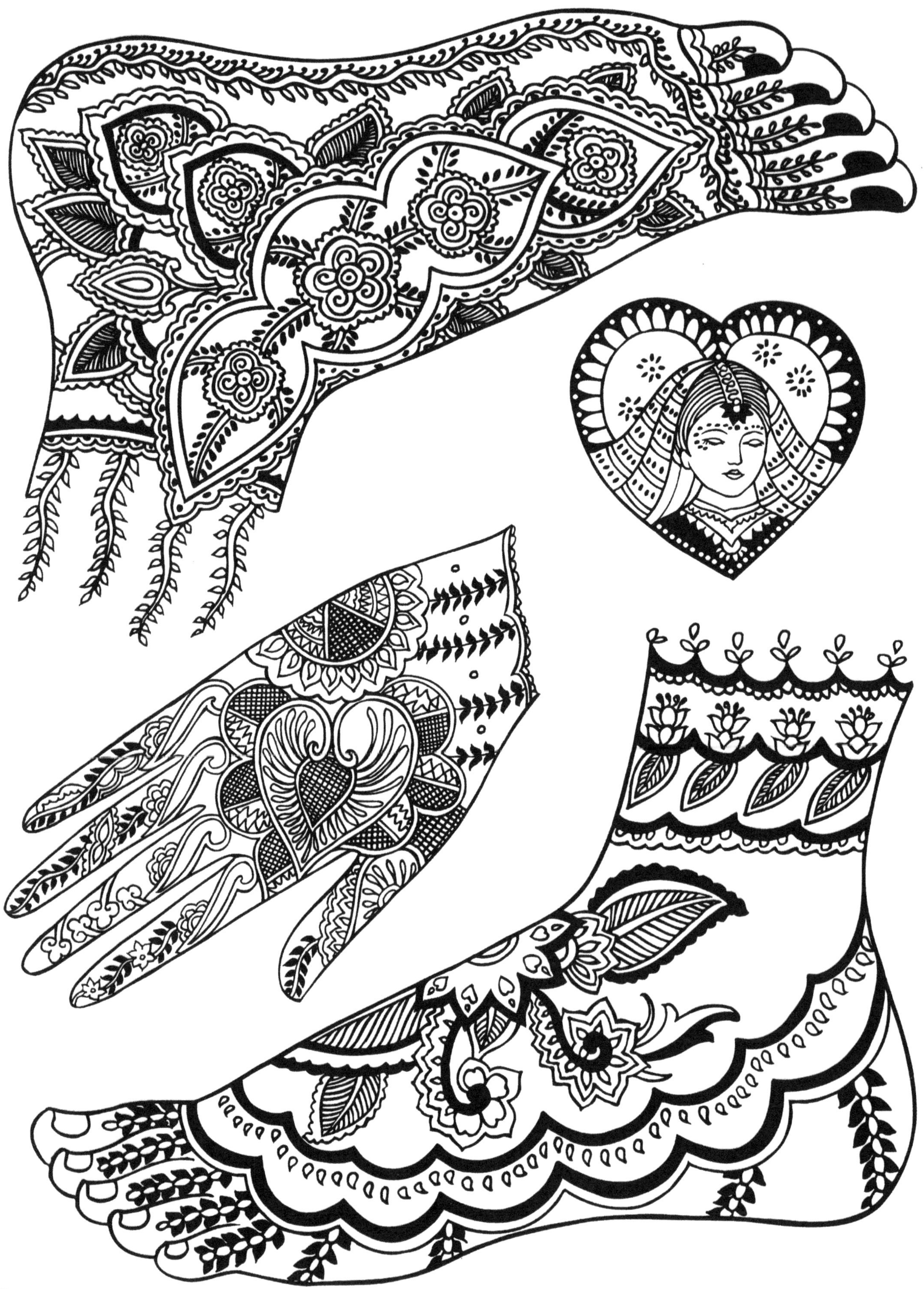

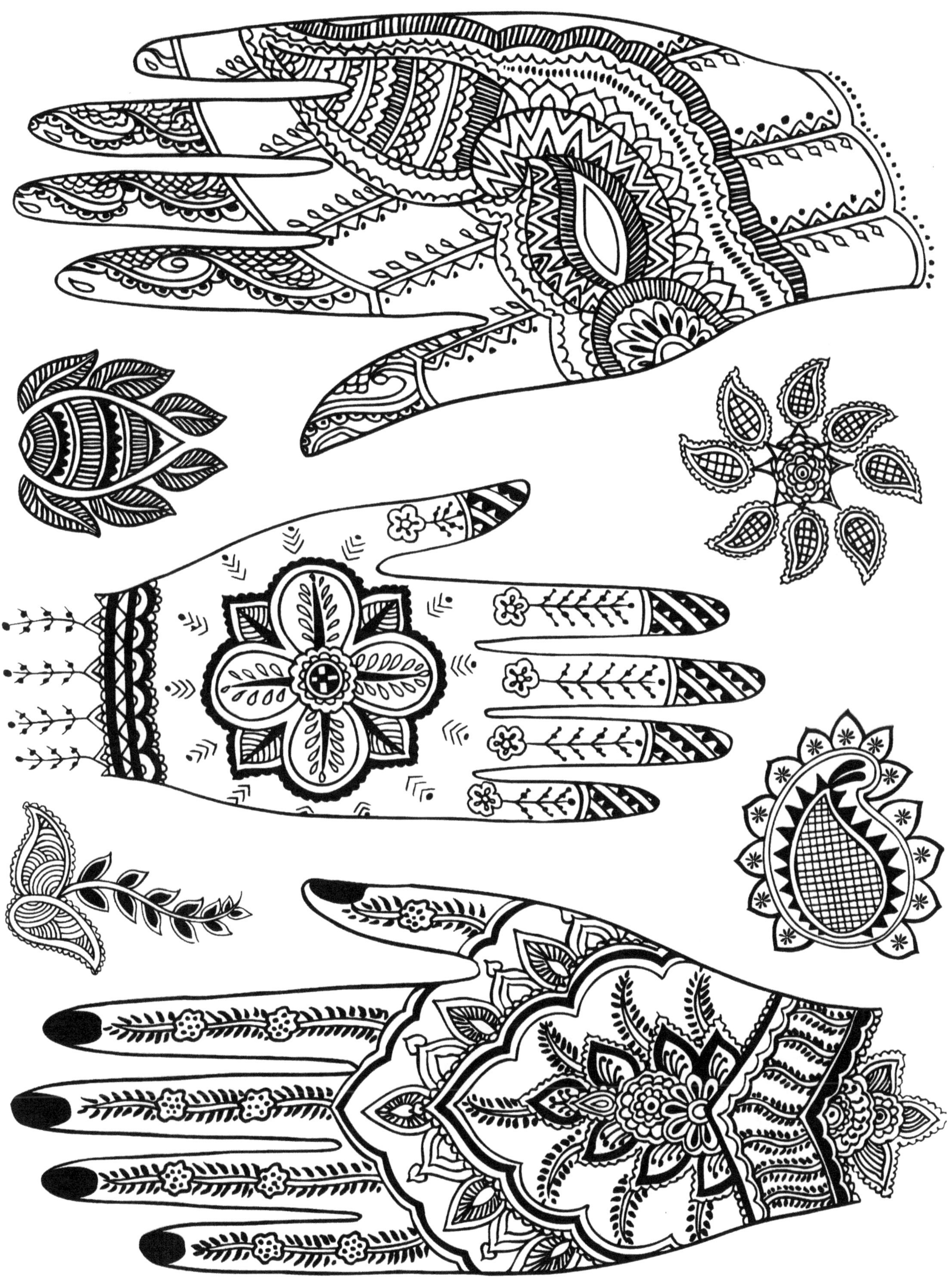

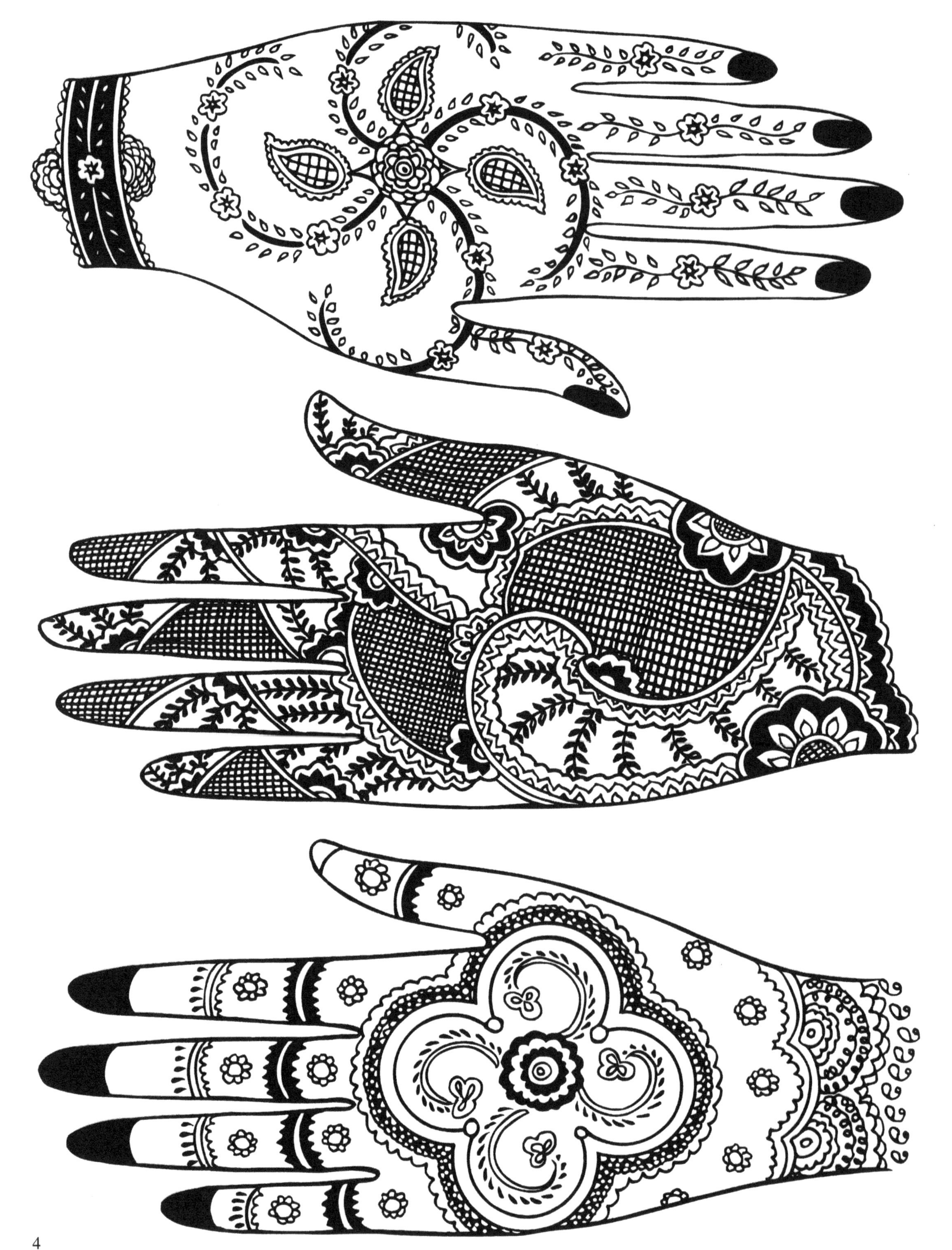

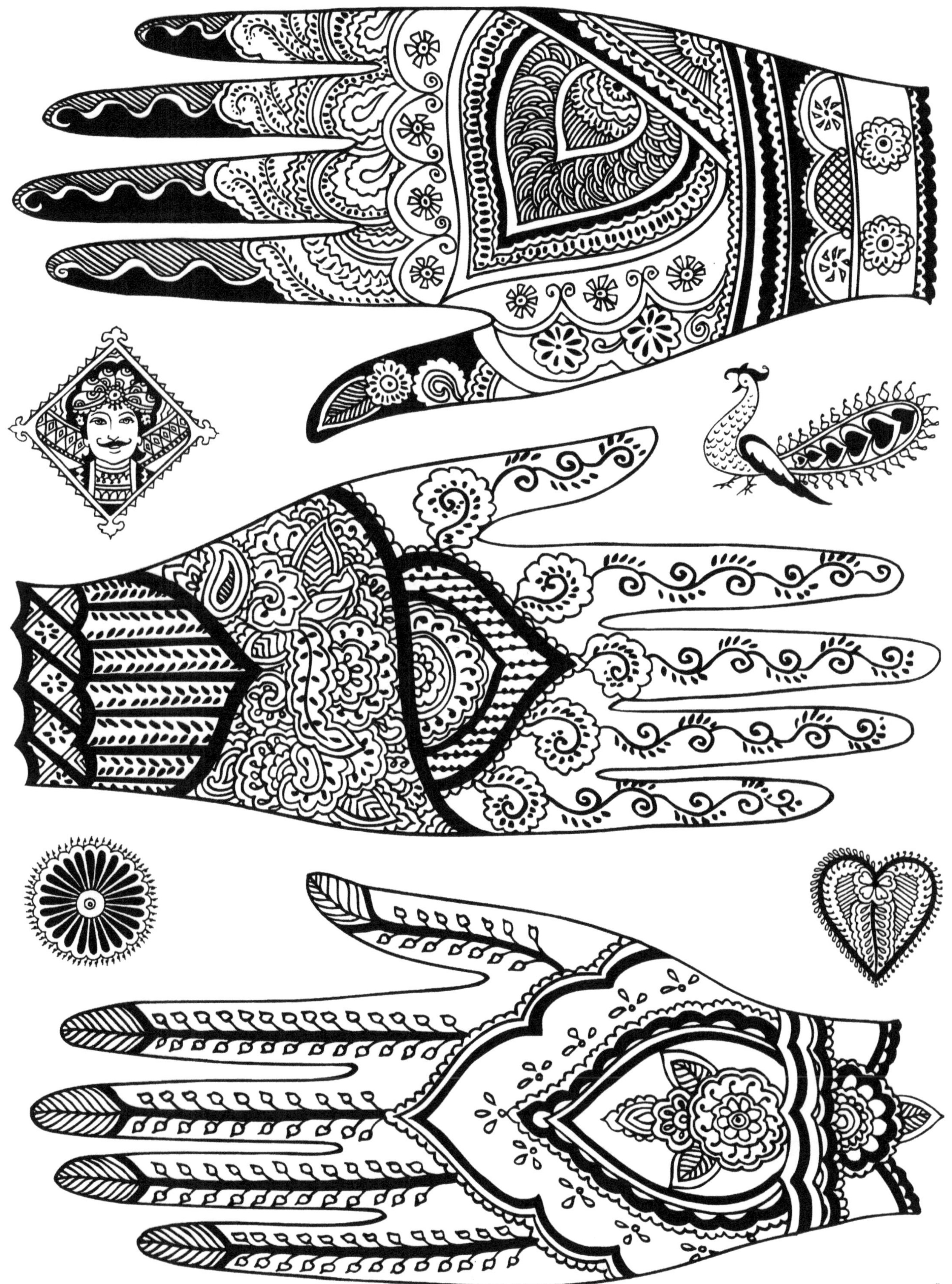

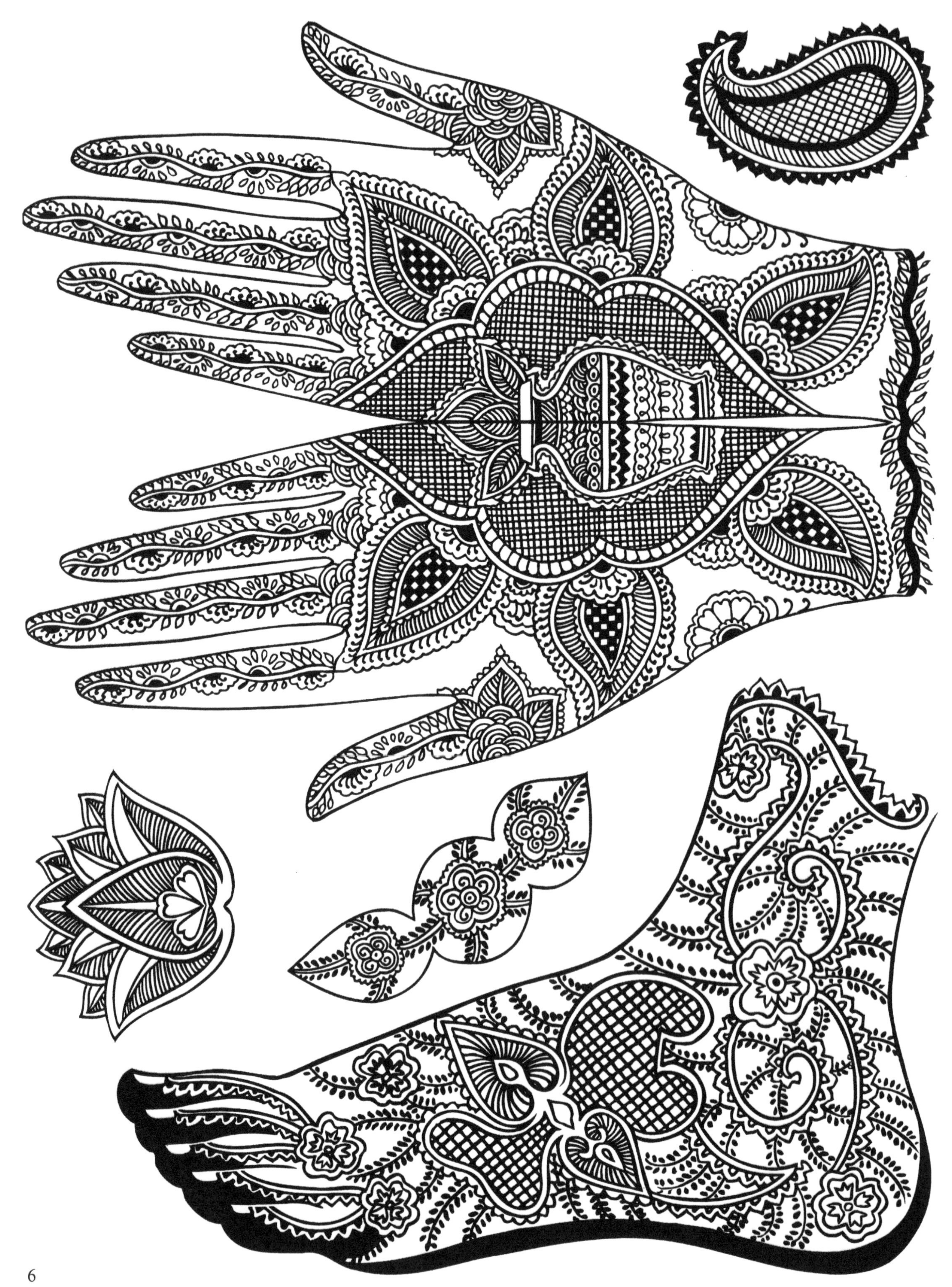

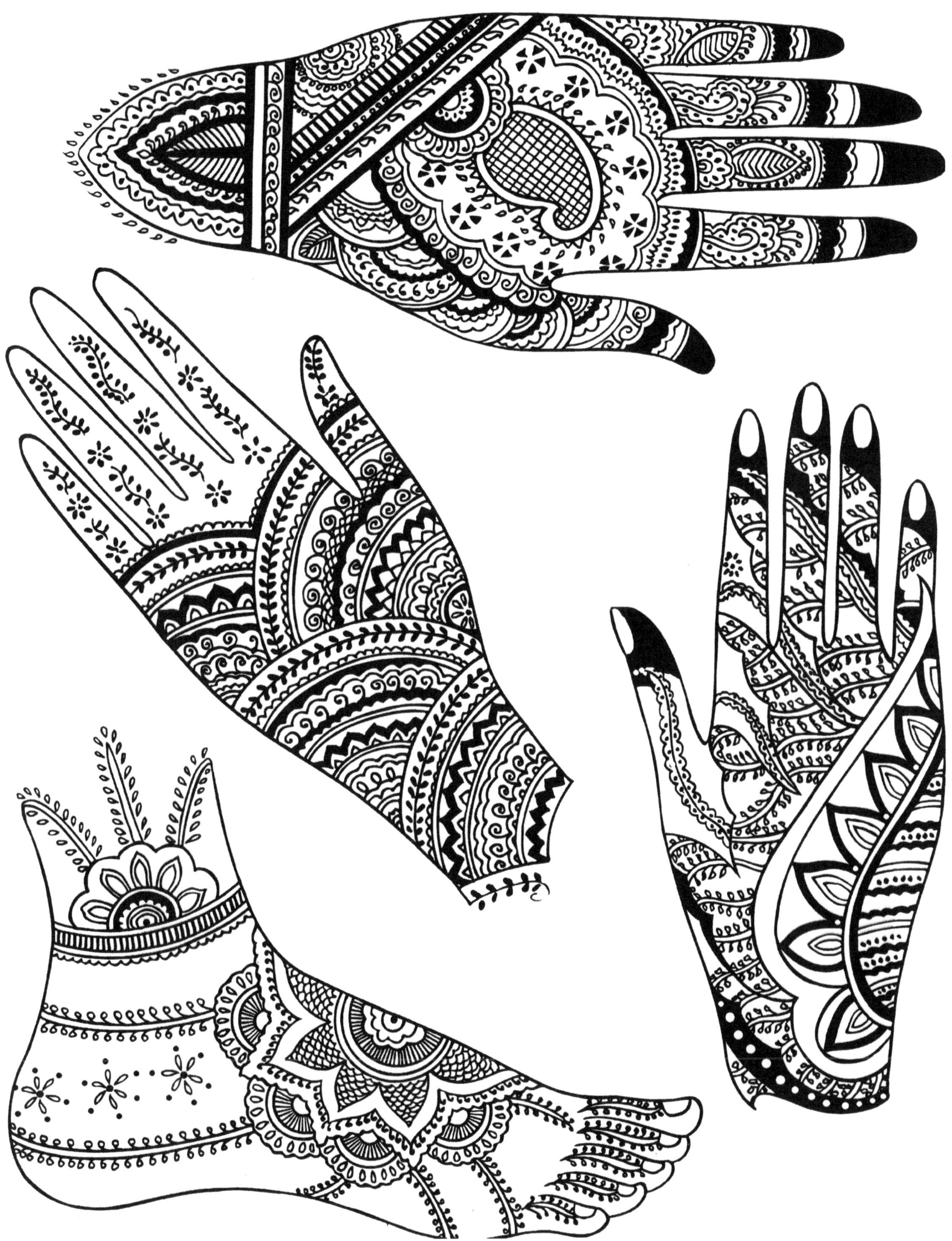

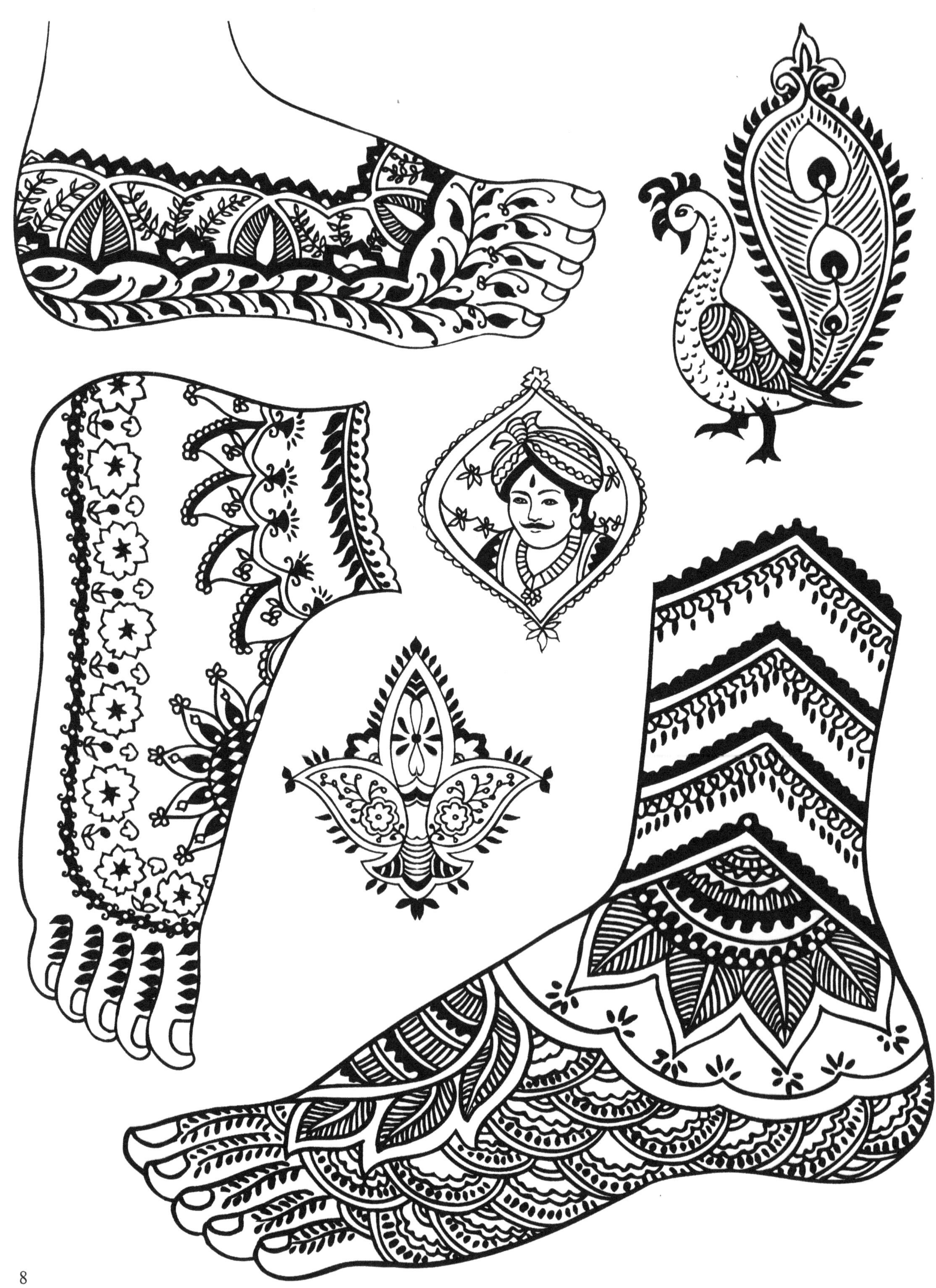

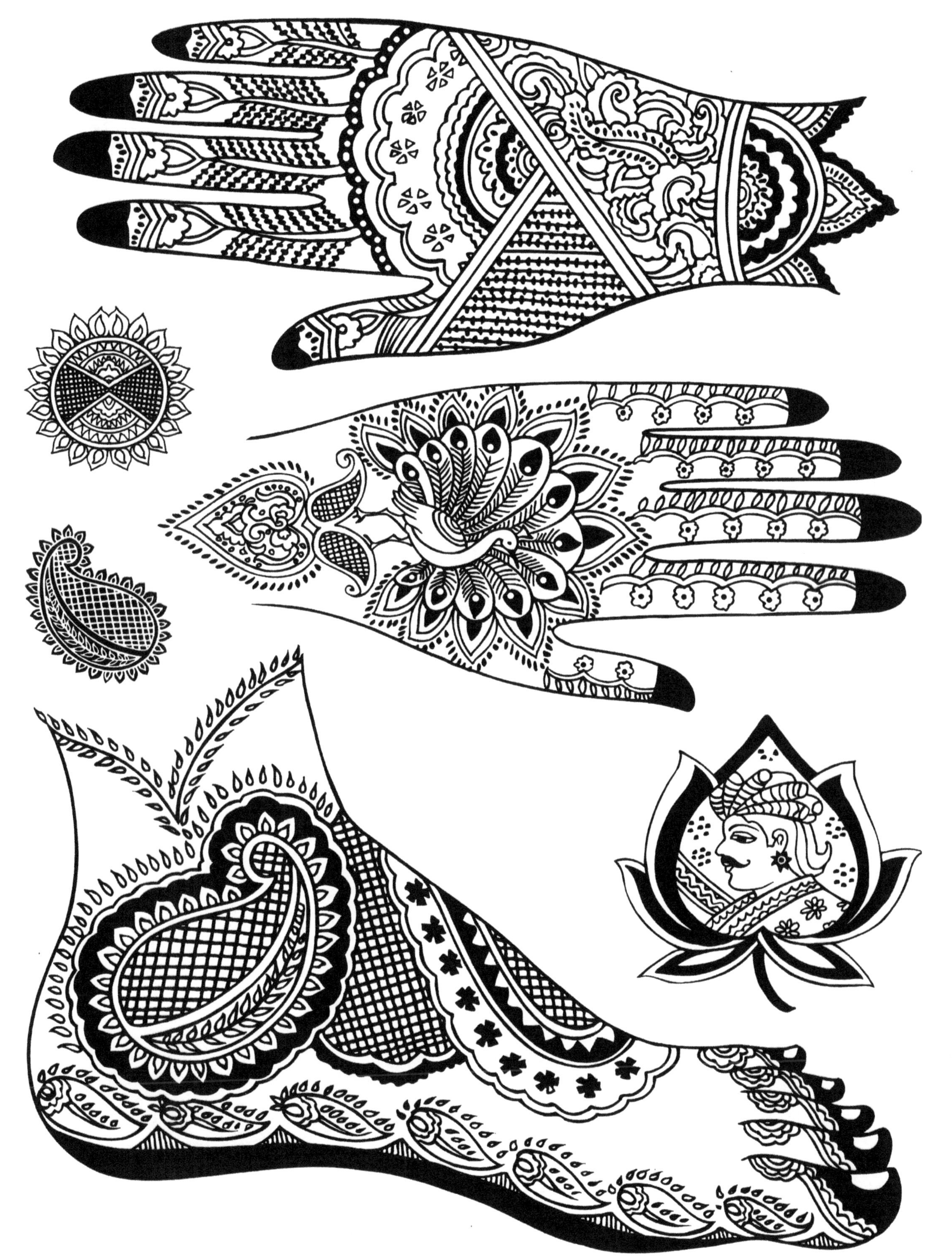

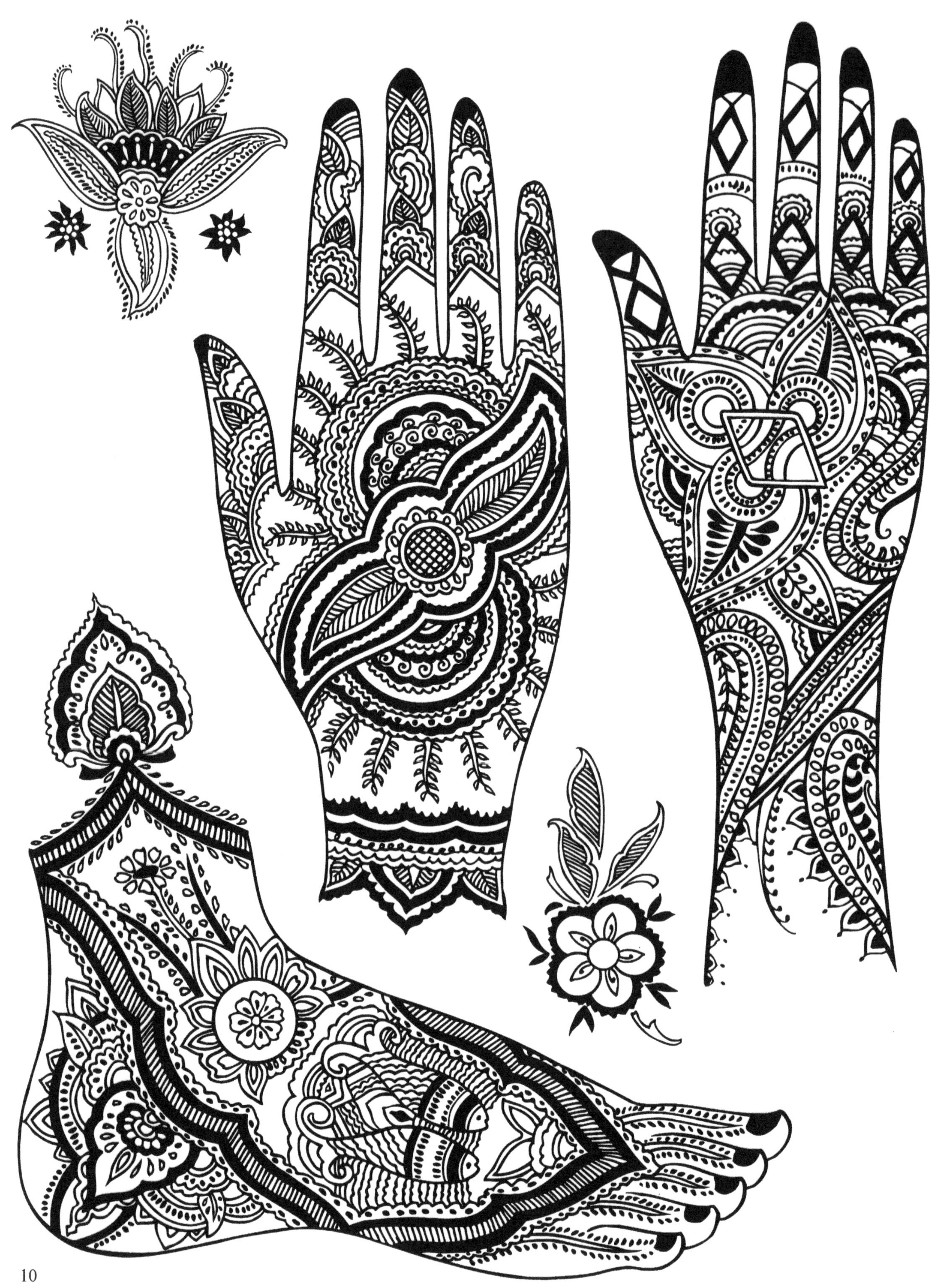

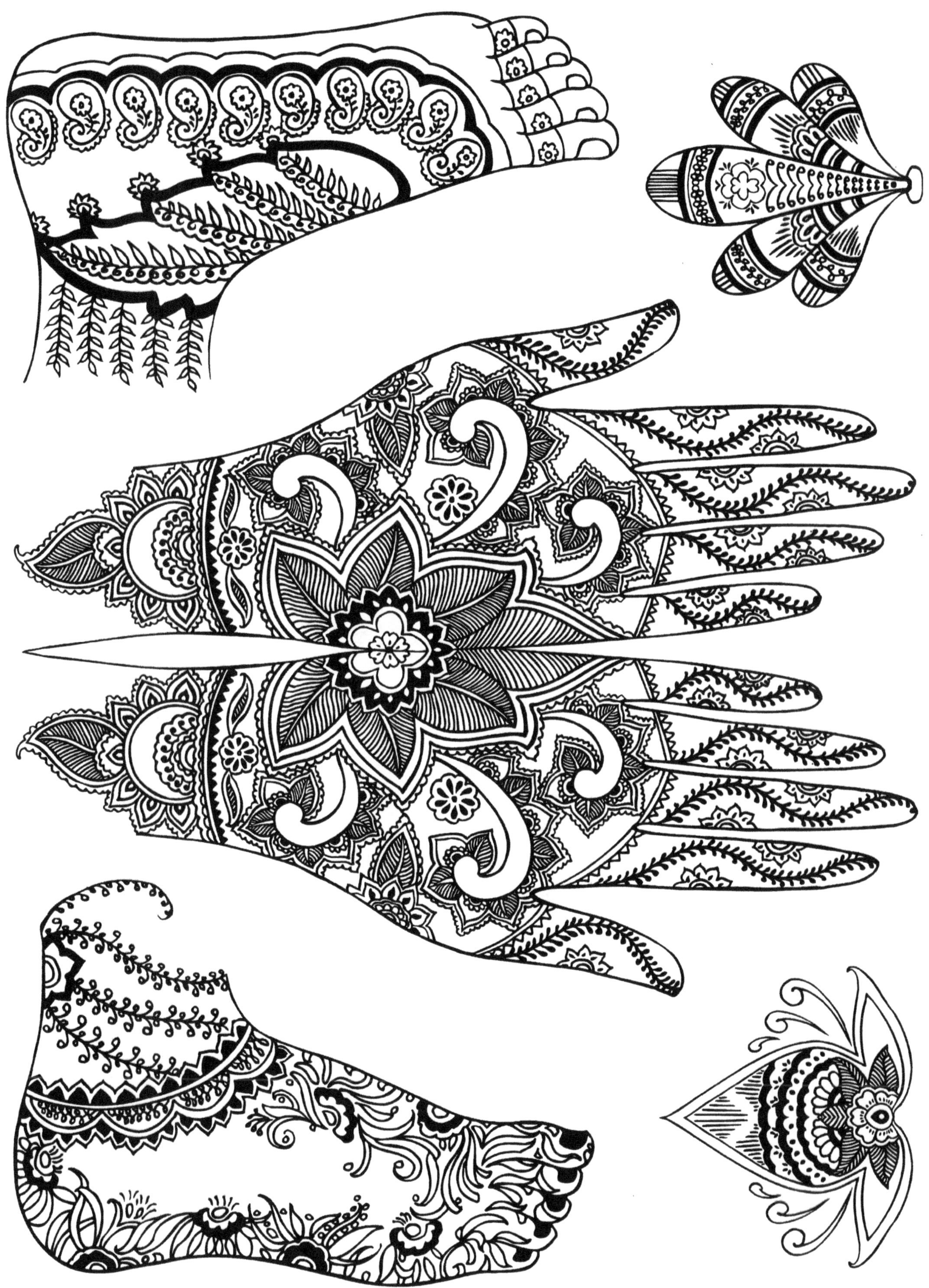

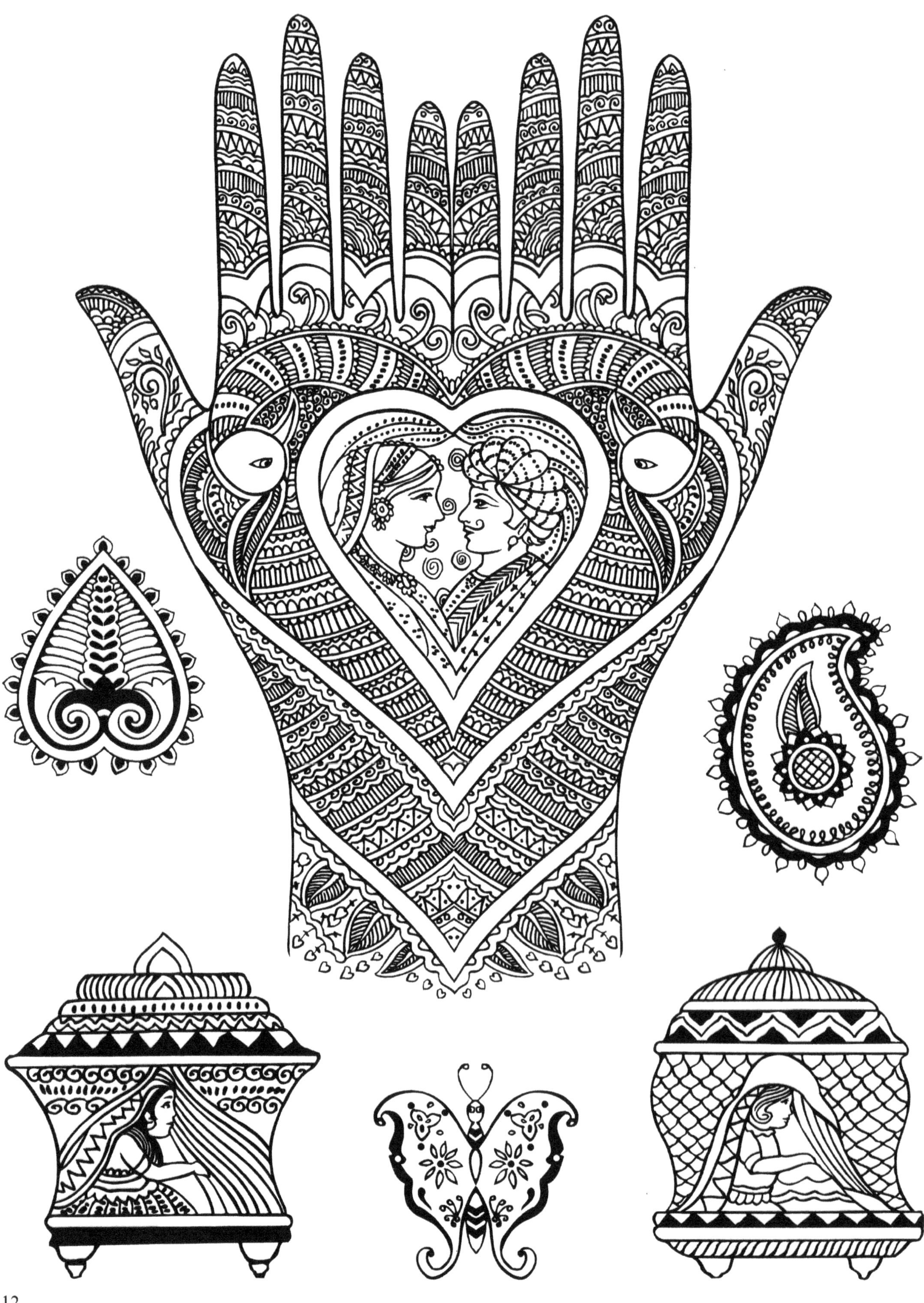

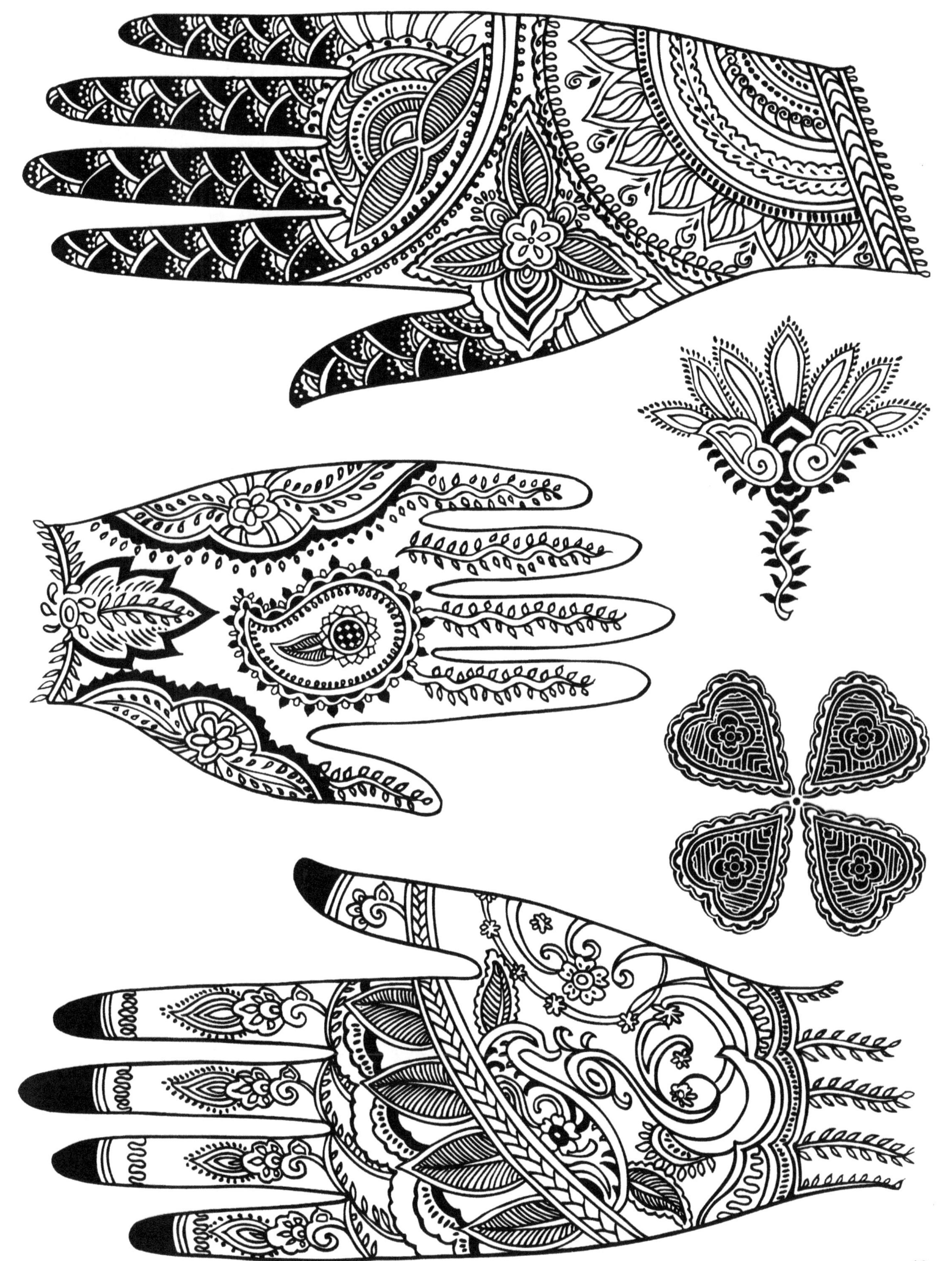

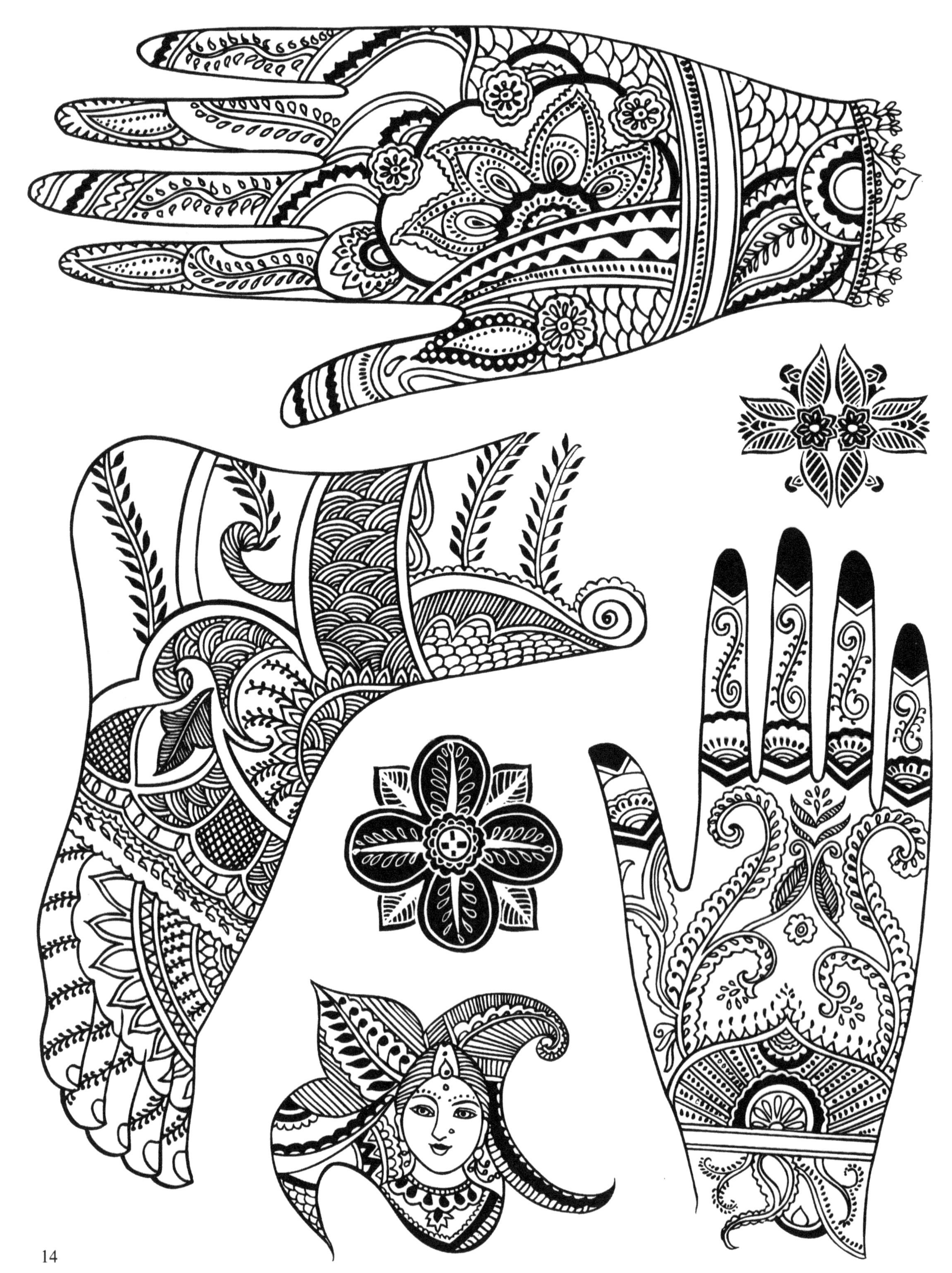

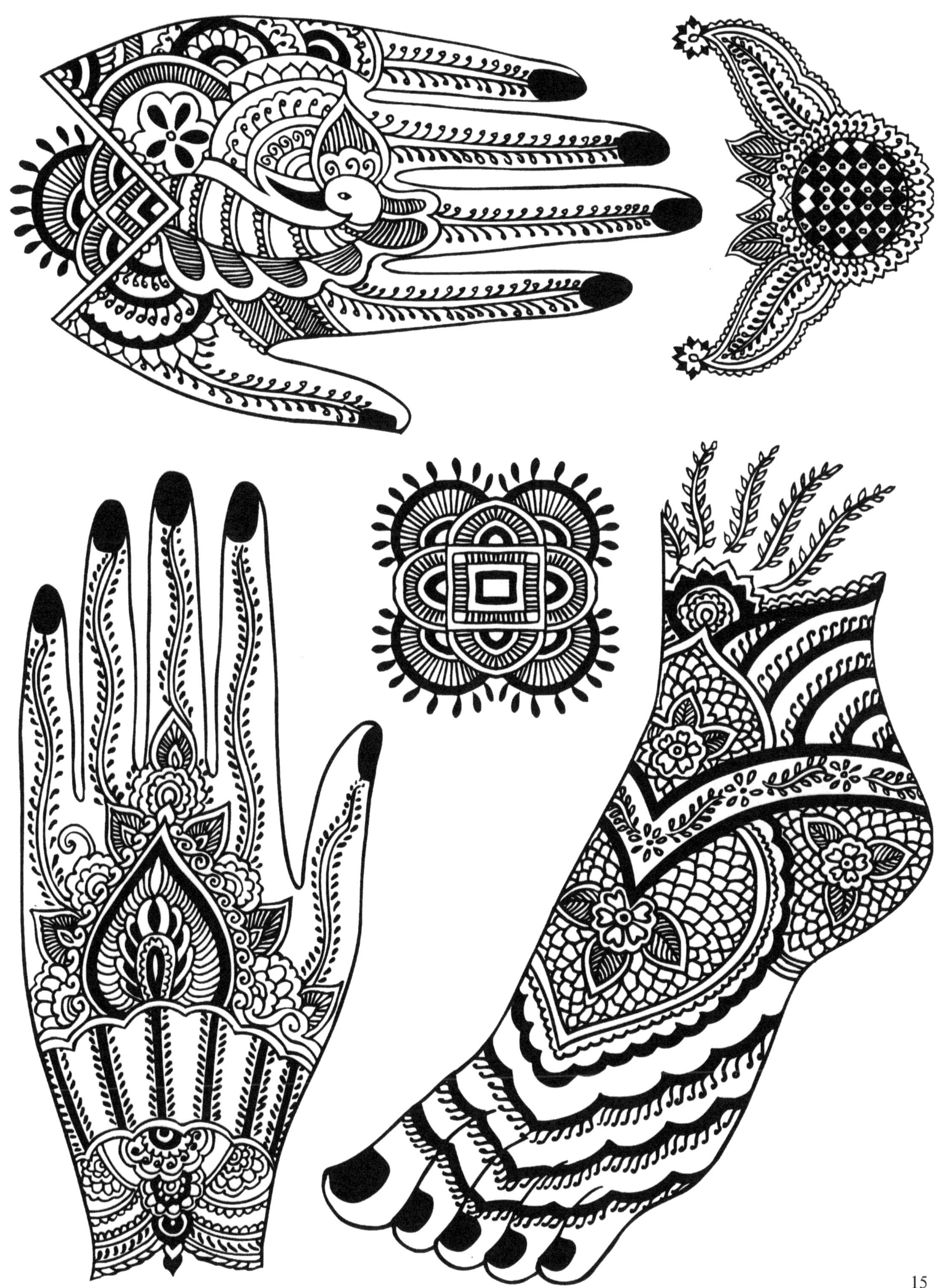

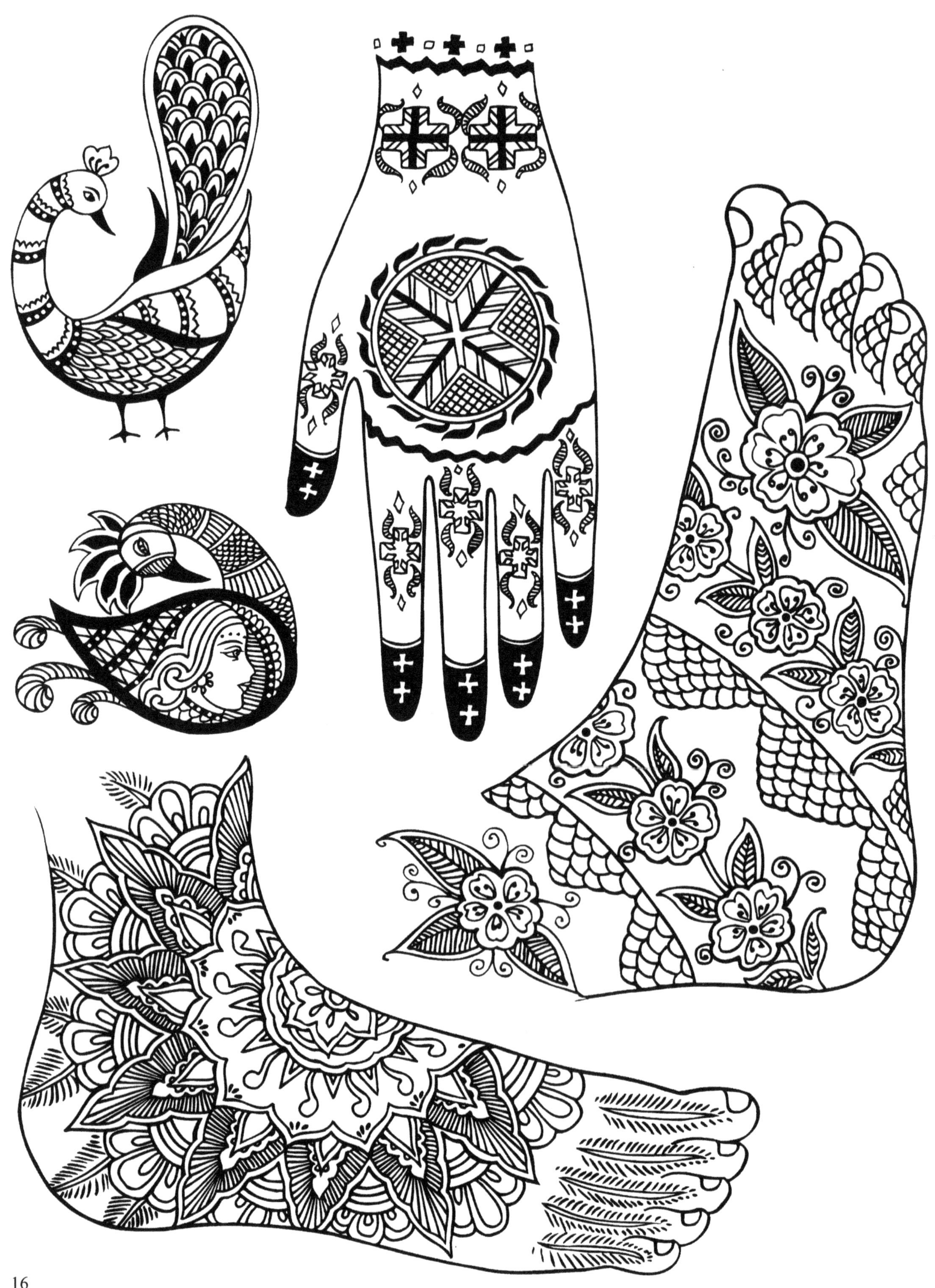

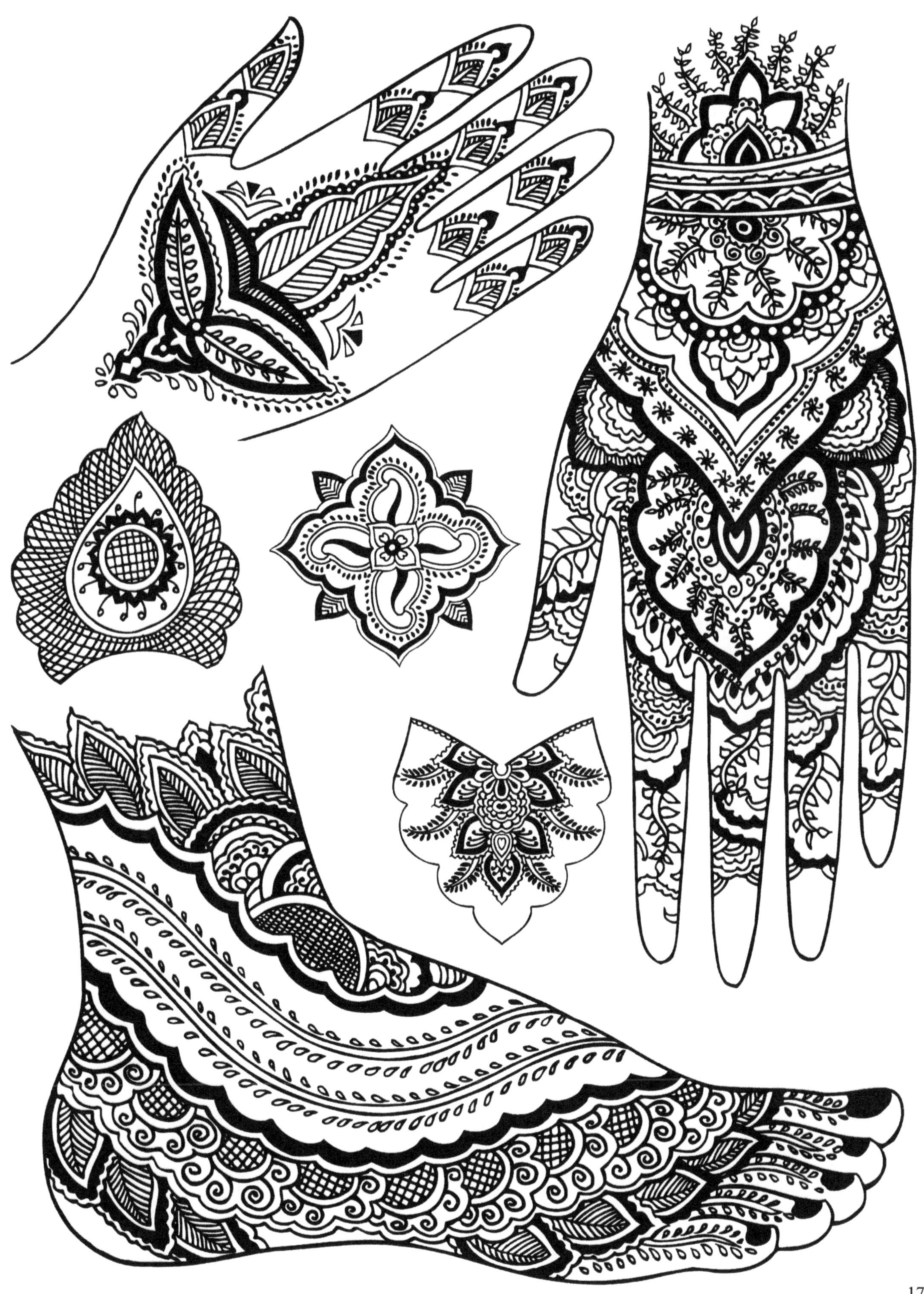

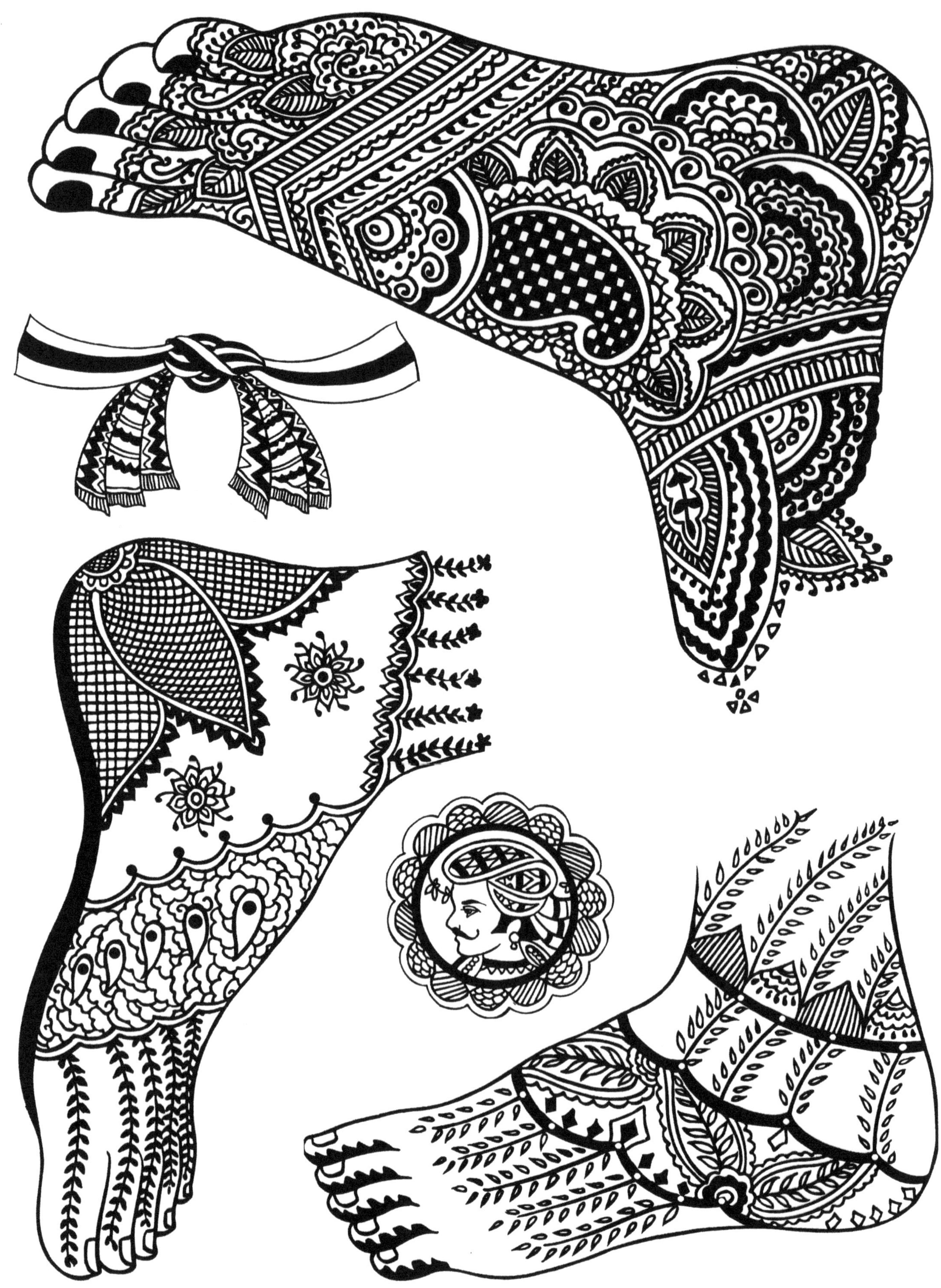

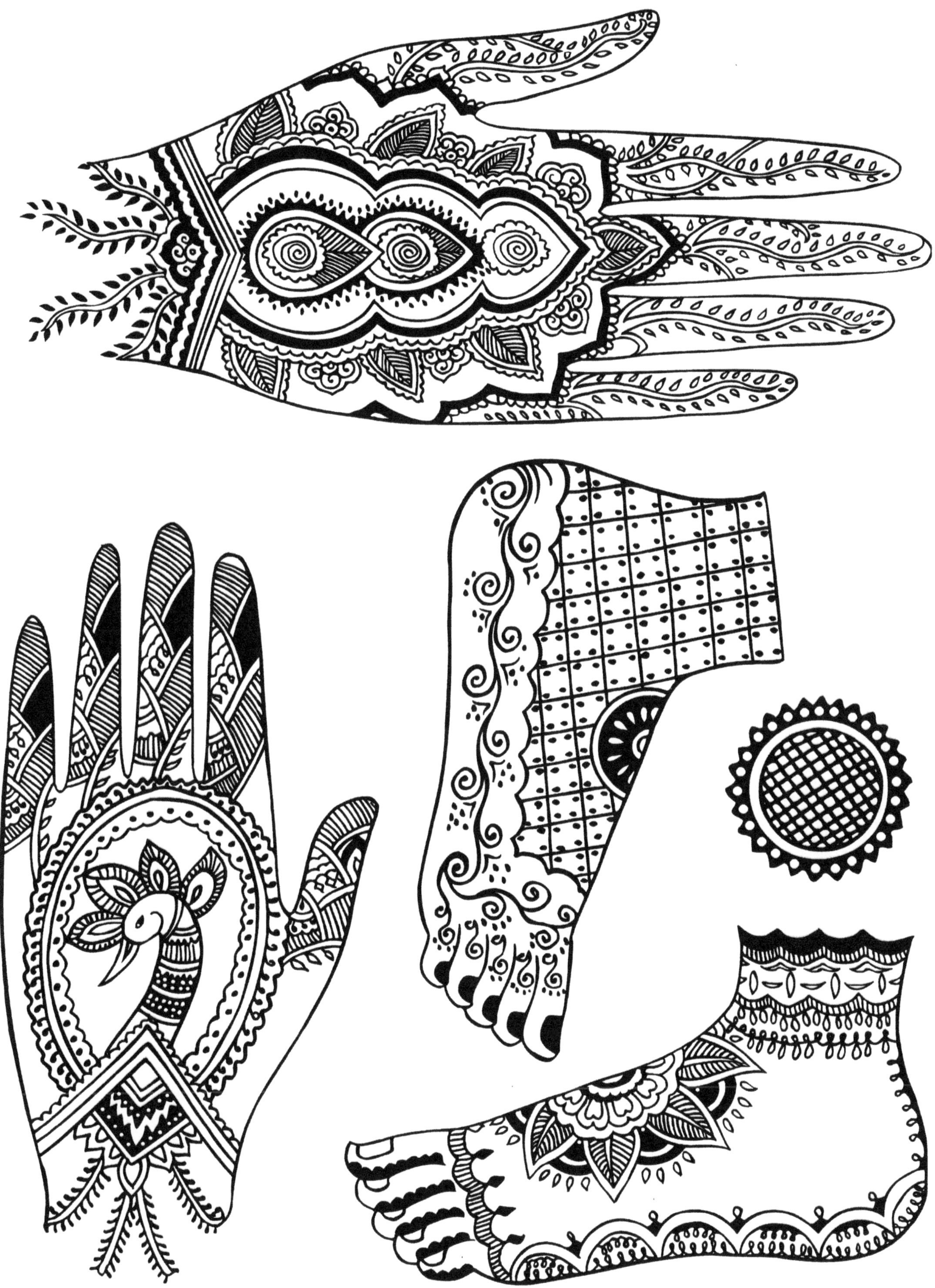

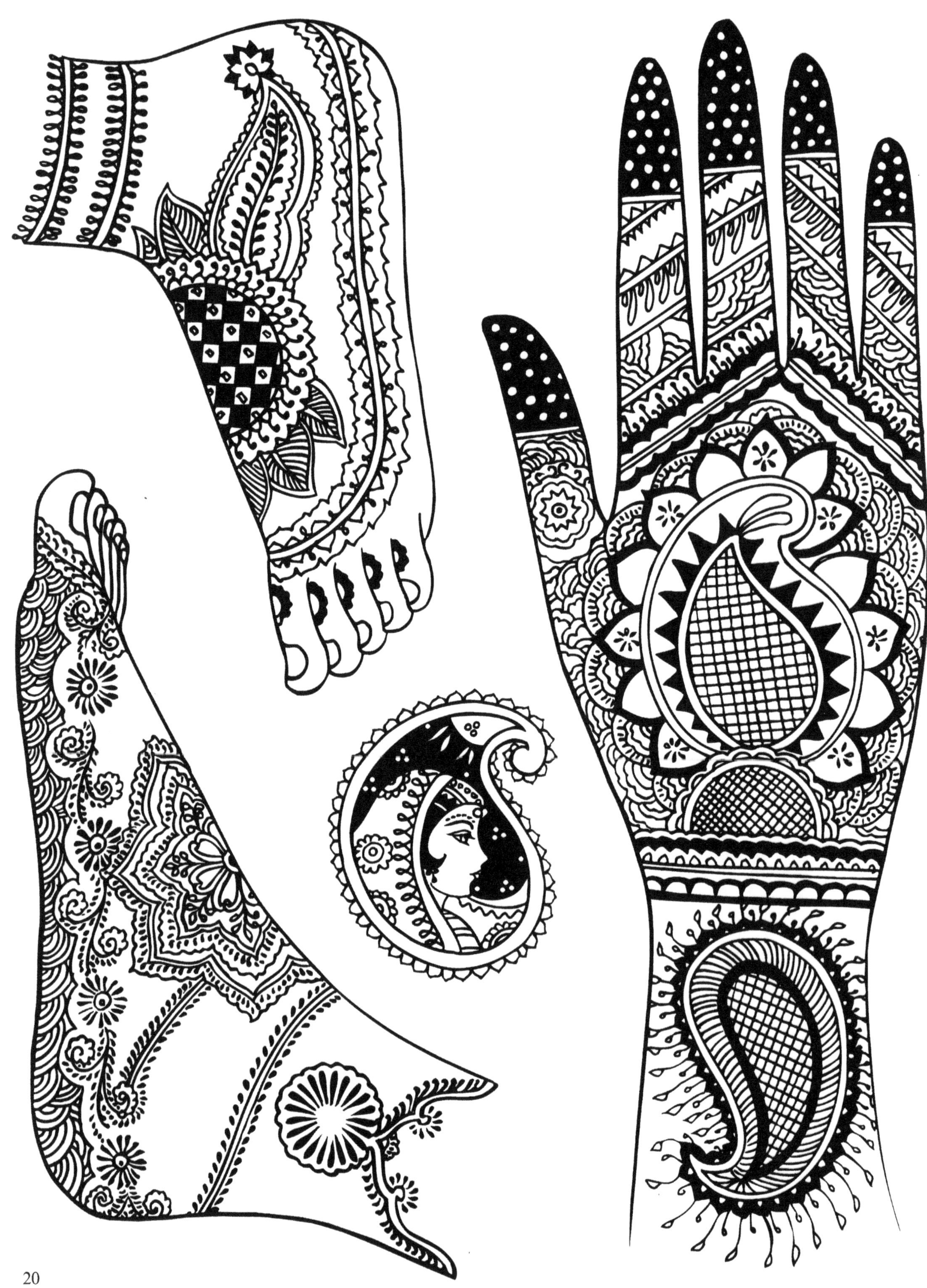

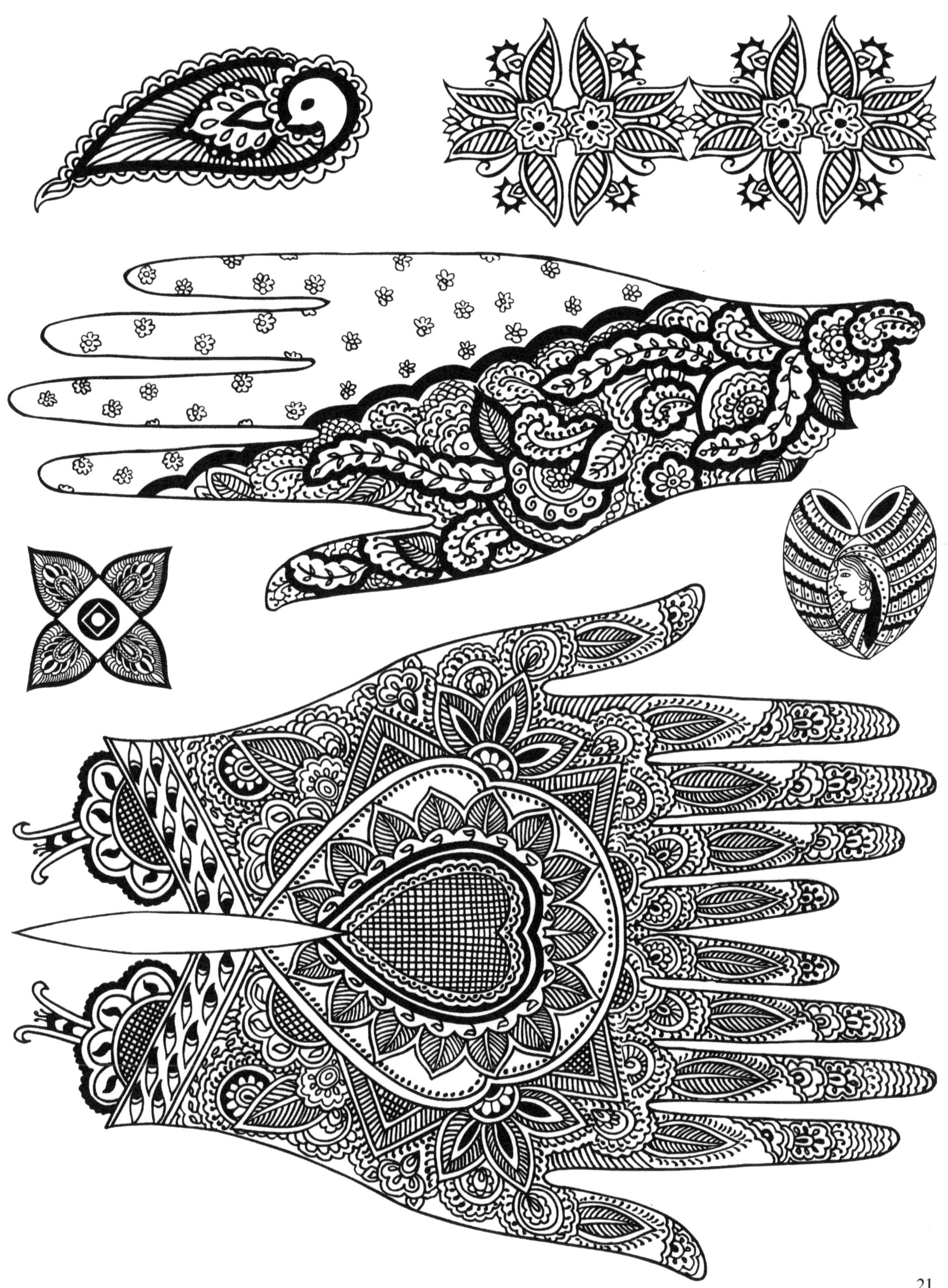

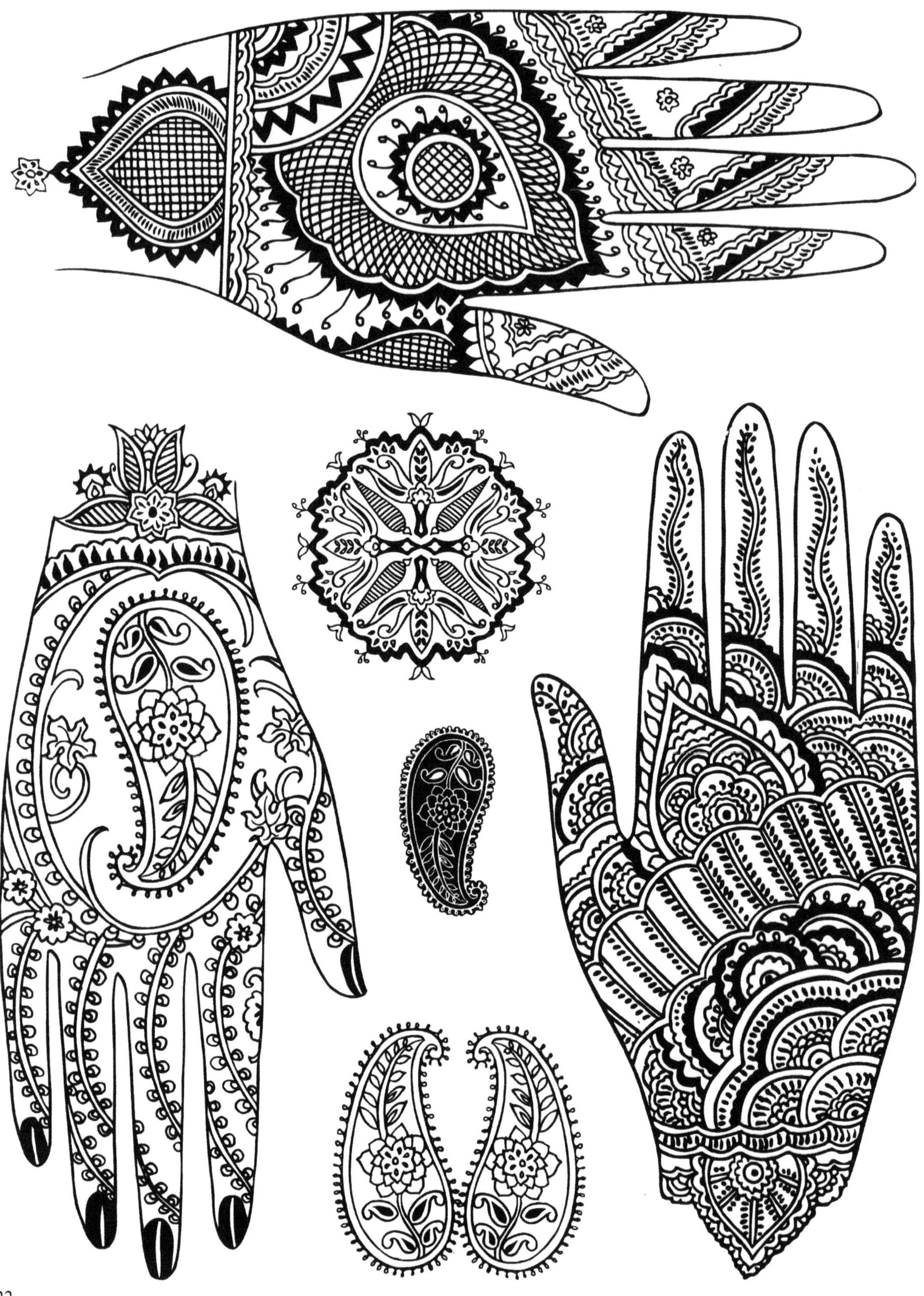

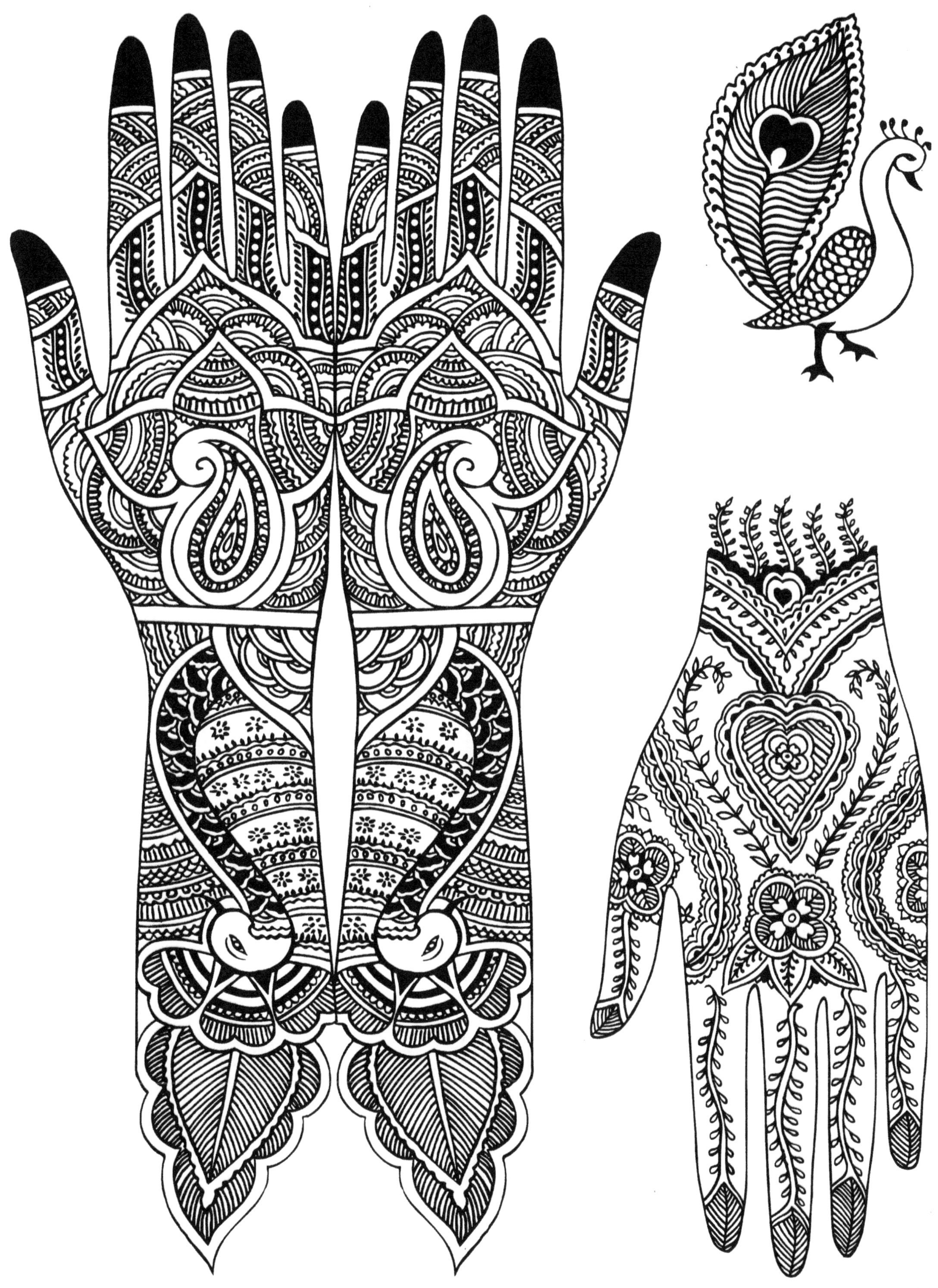

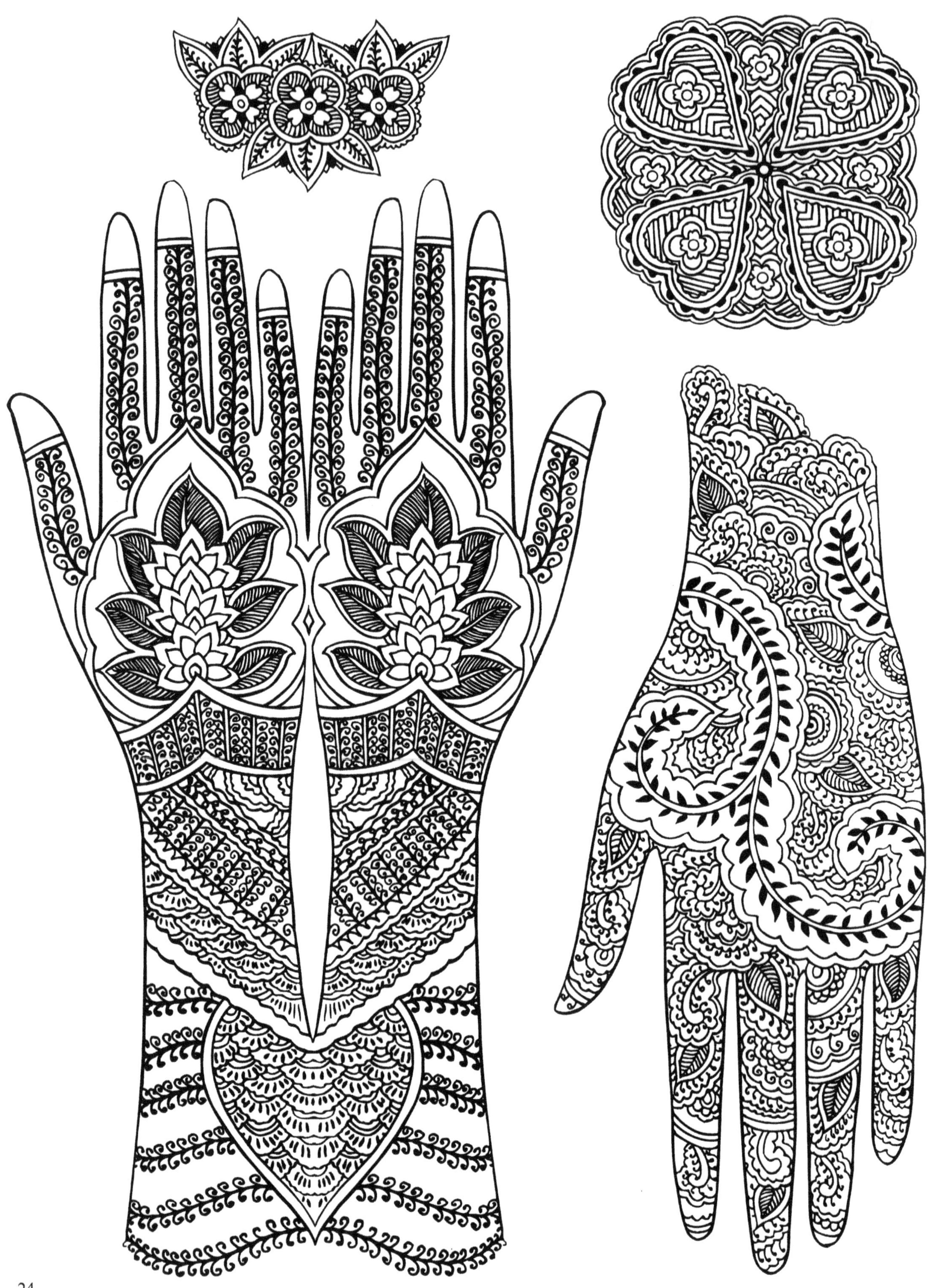

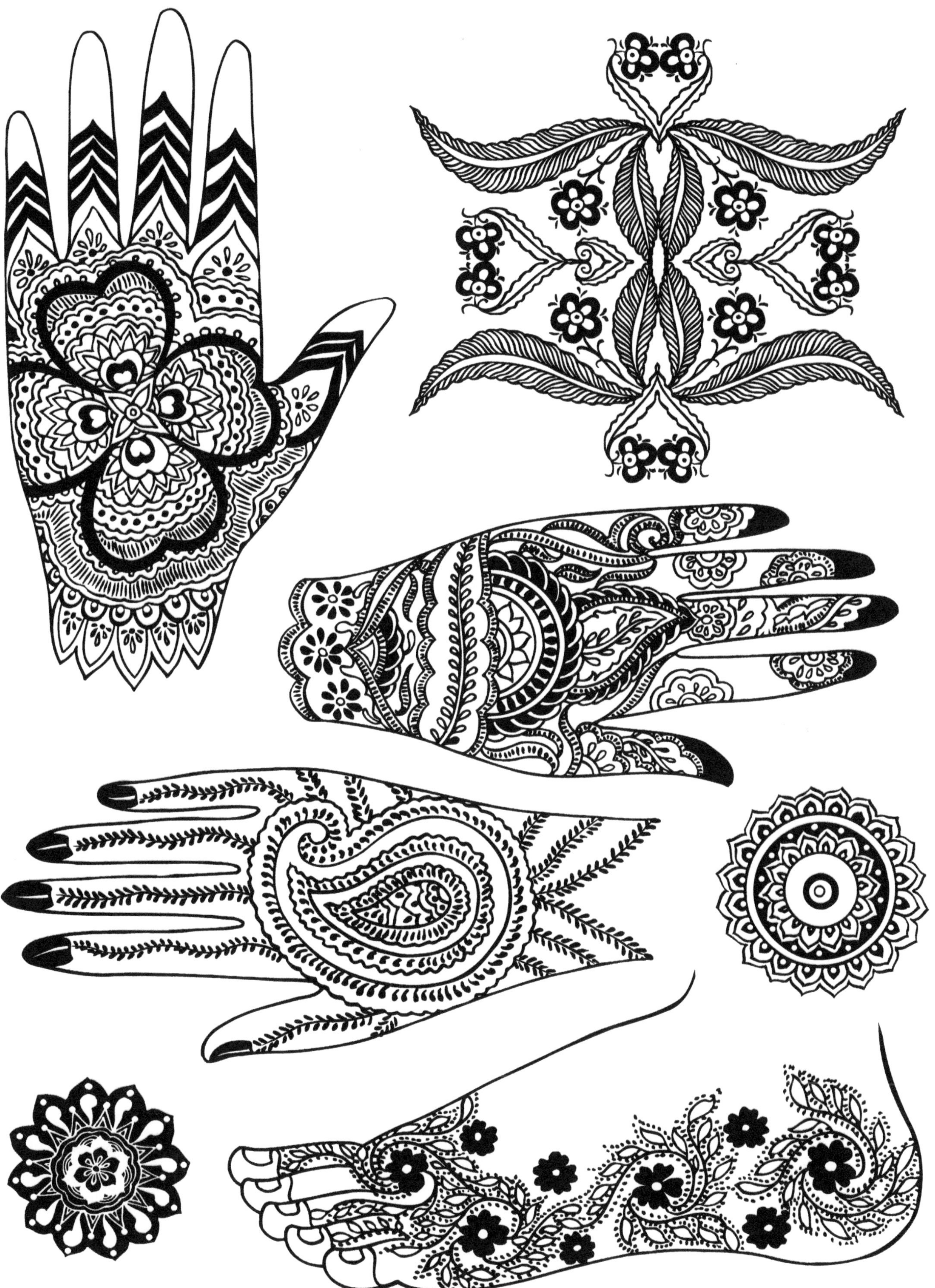

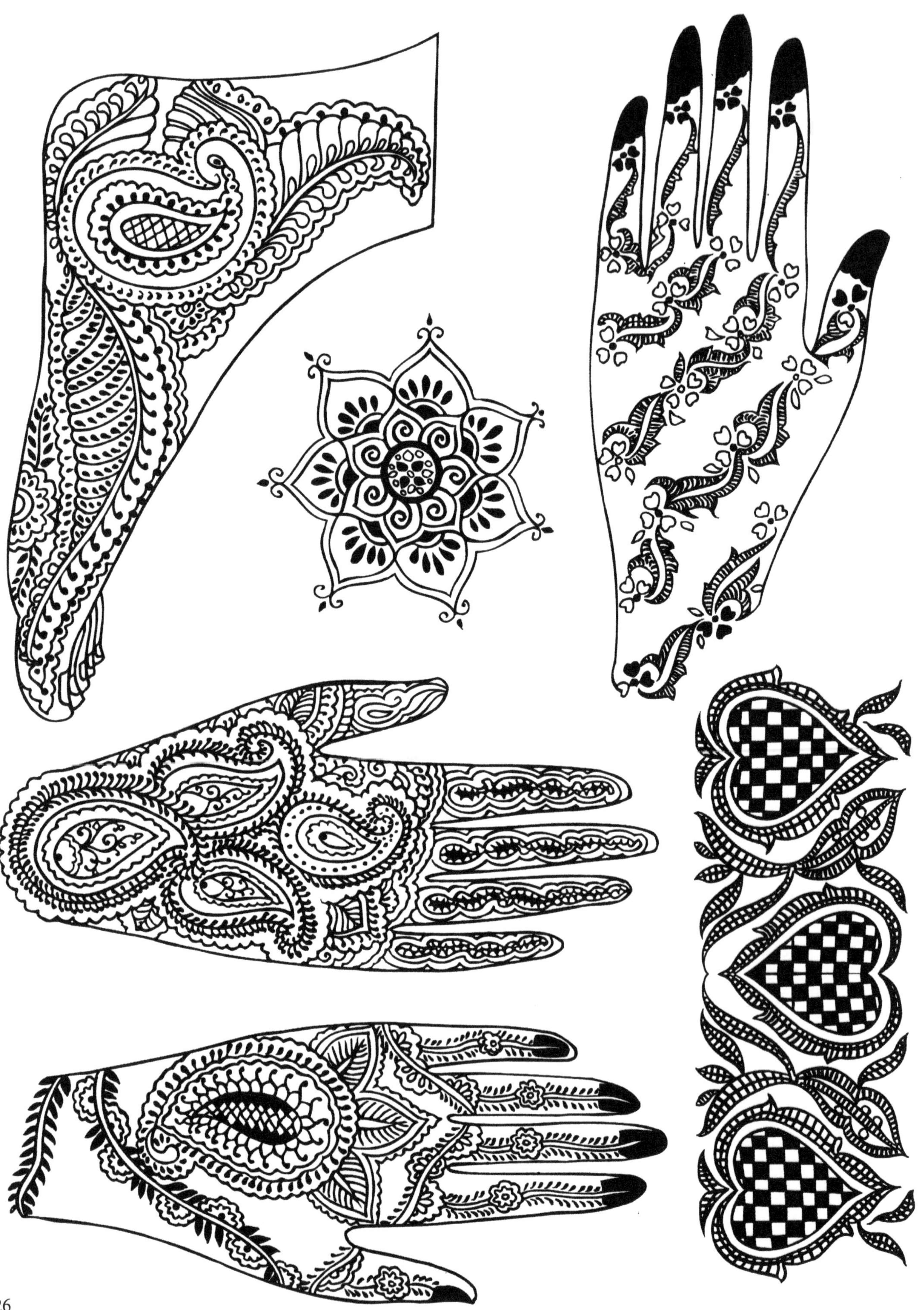

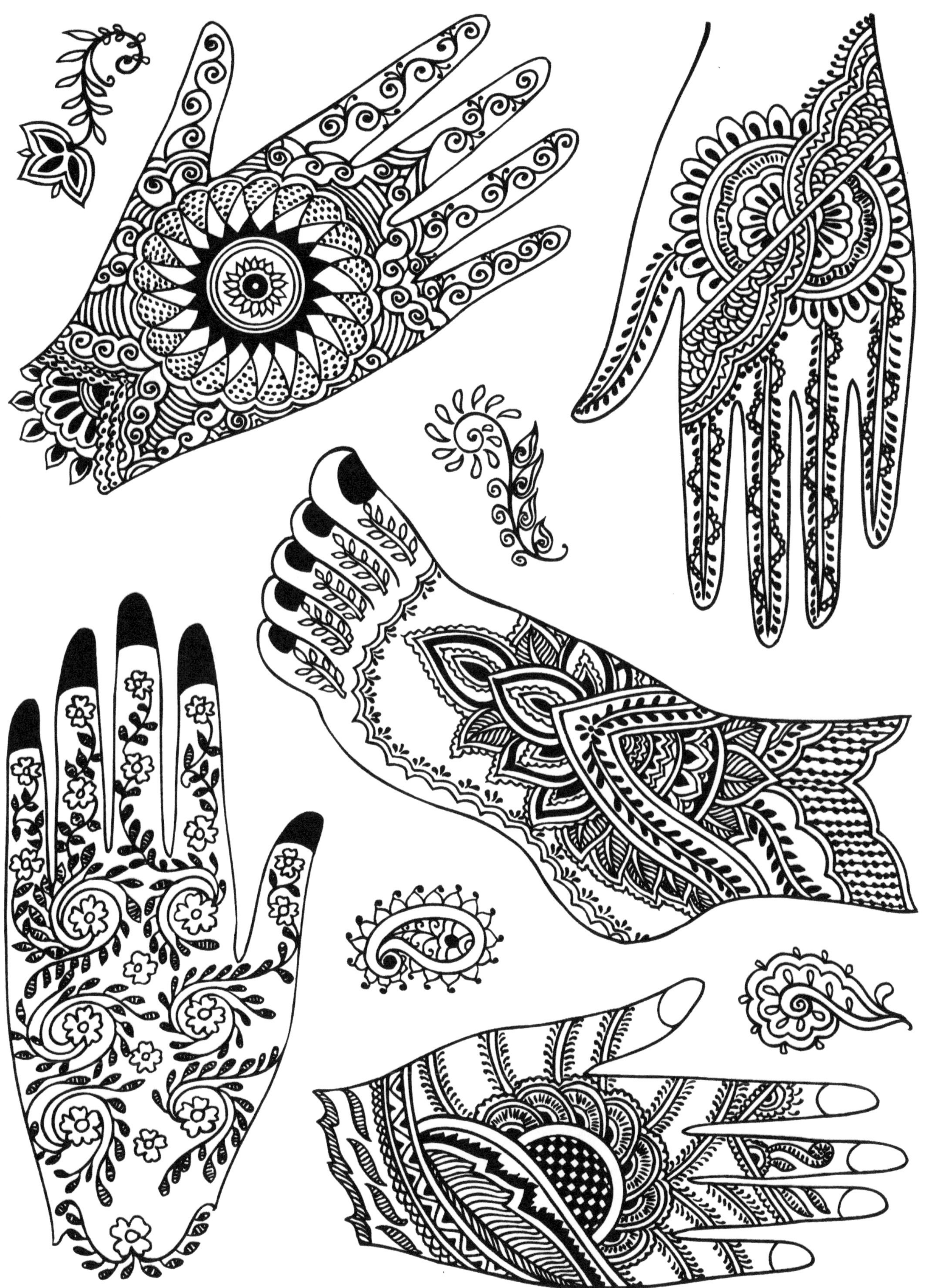

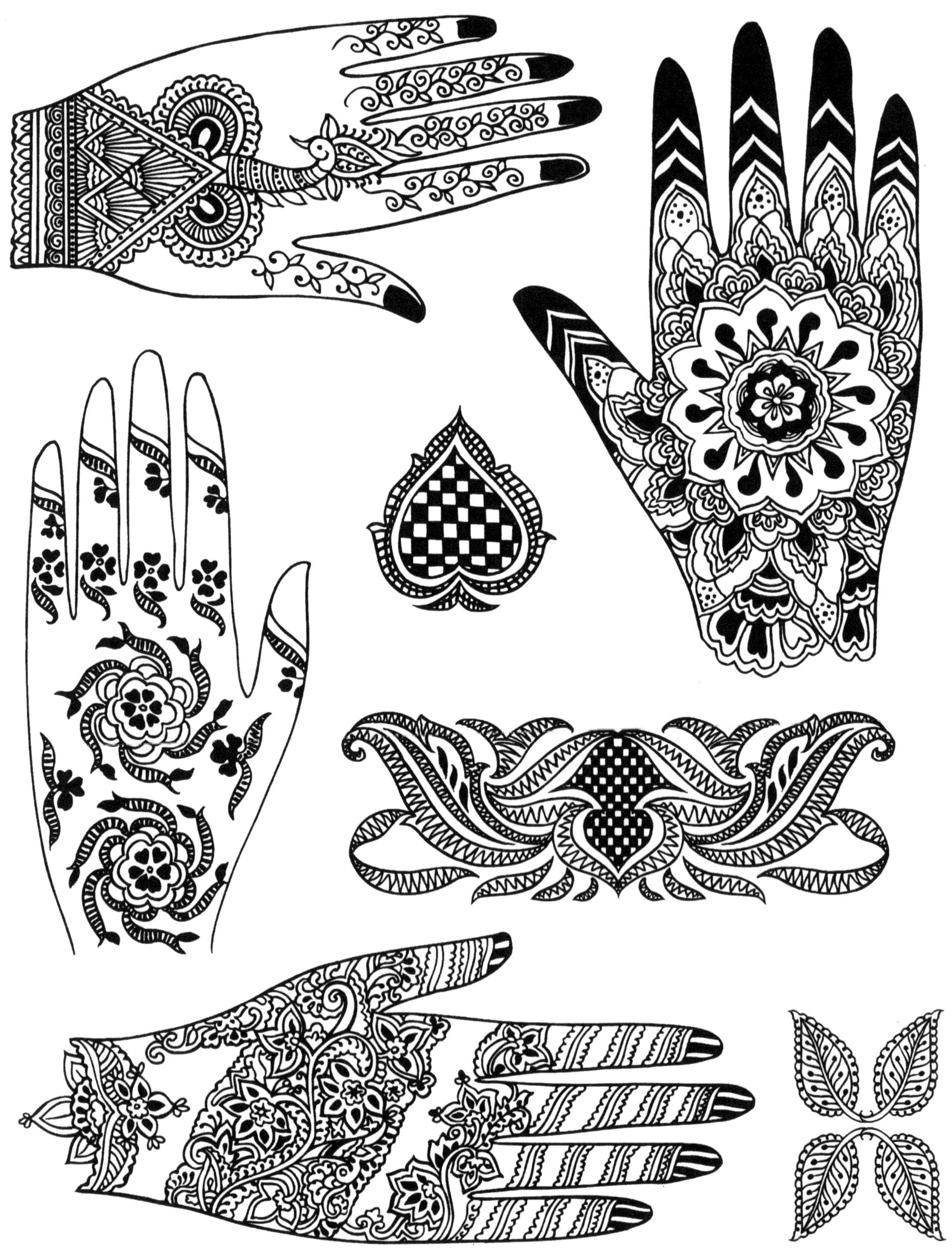

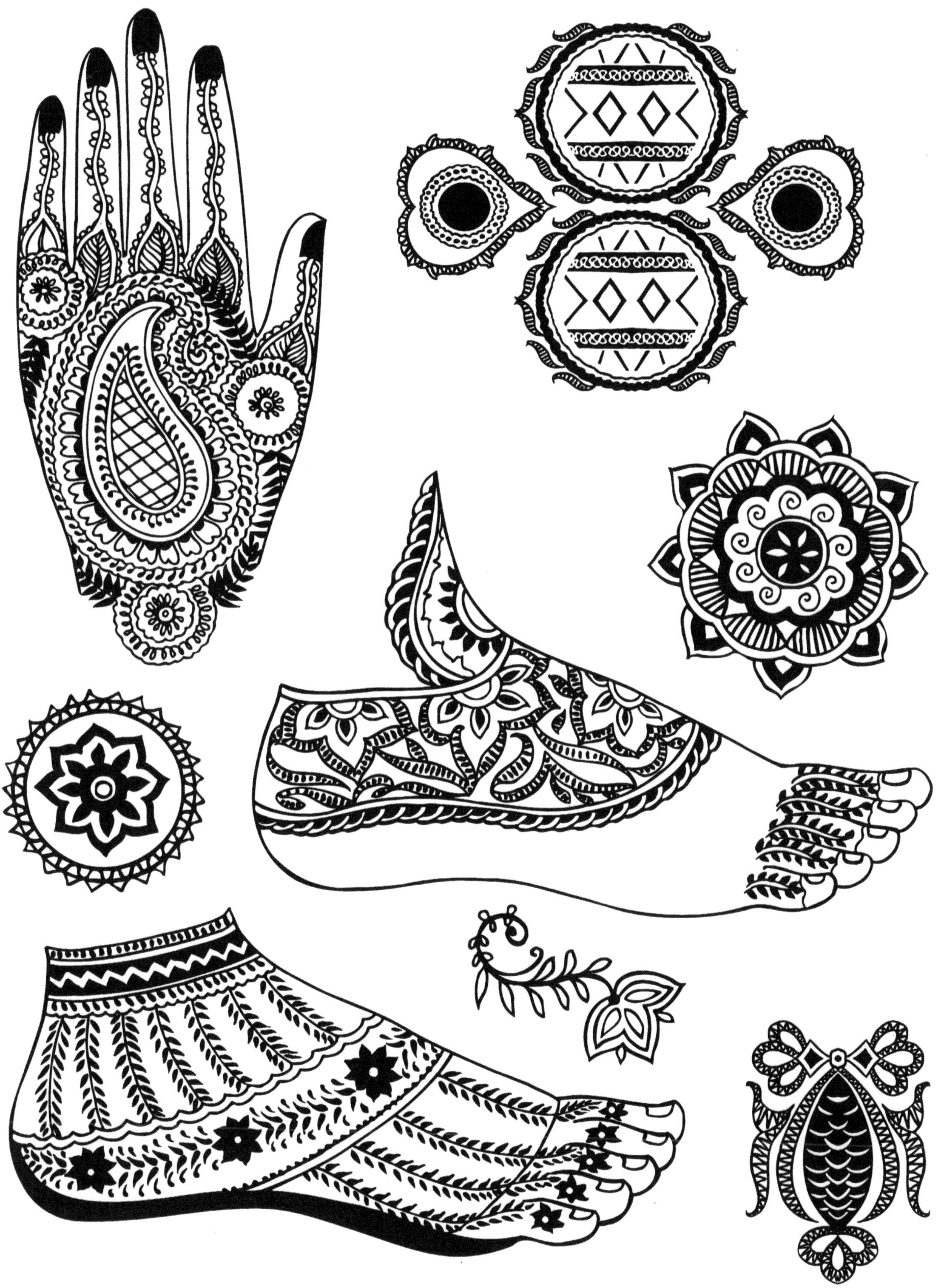

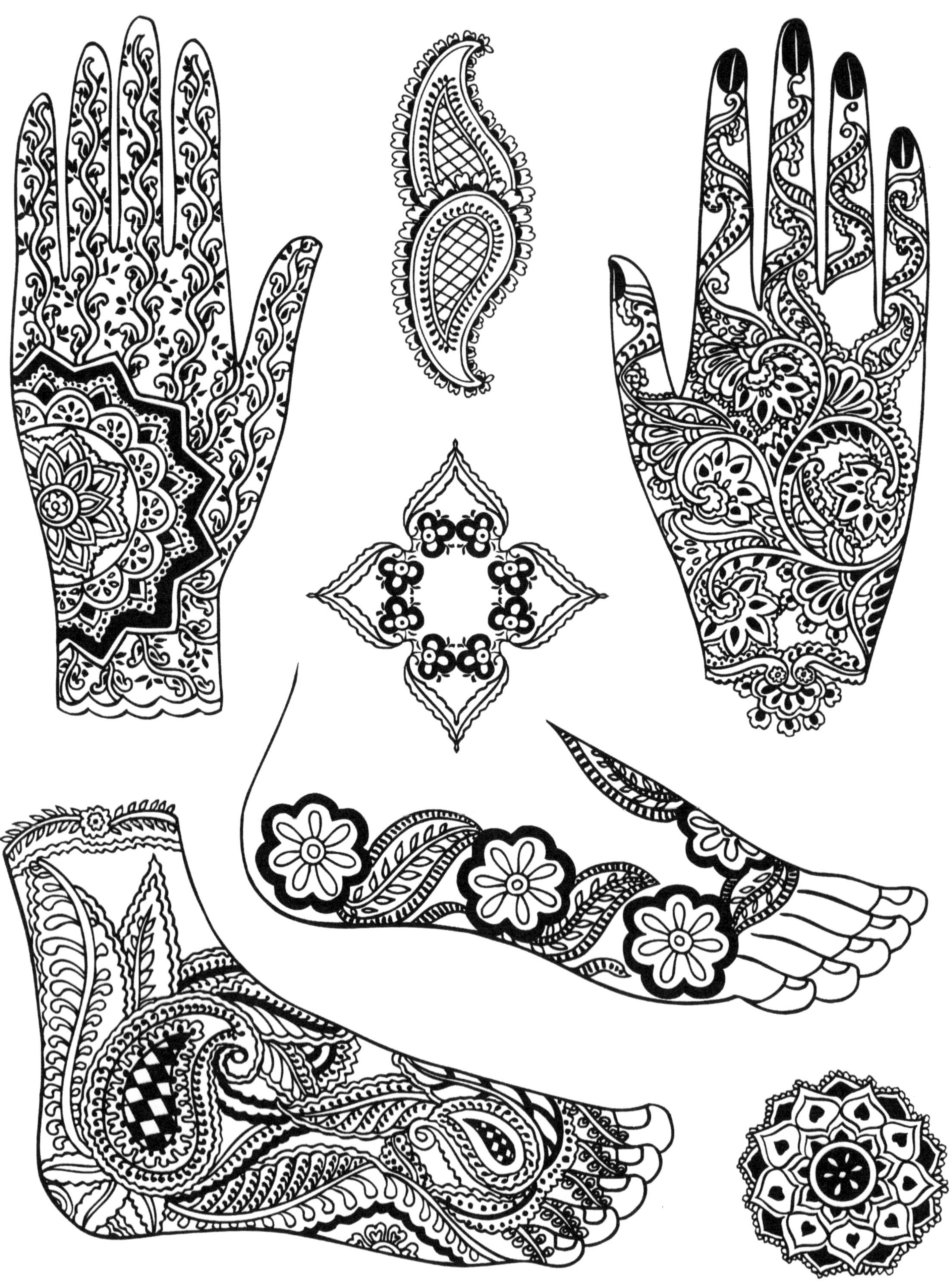